Economics in a Nutshell

The Political Destruction of Free Enterprise

G. Peter Trygstad

 www.trafford.com

North America & international
toll-free: 1 888 232 4444 (USA & Canada)
phone: 250 383 6864 ♦ fax: 812 355 4082

Dedication

This manuscript is a product of a working life pursuing knowledge and an understanding of the physical and political world. I could not have written it as a young man. Experience is the greatest contributor. I also could not have written it without the patience and understanding of my working wife Elnora who encouraged her retired husband to assemble some of his written political musings into a coherent story for publishing. I dedicate this book to her.

G. Peter Trygstad

Economics in a Nutshell
G. Peter Trygstad

First Law

In free enterprise the competition for sales will drive prices downward until all products are sold. Prices can fall no further.

Second Law

In free enterprise the competition for employment will drive wages downward until all labor is hired. Wages can fall no further.

Third Law

In free enterprise full employment is natural, the production of consumer goods is at its highest, and the buying power of wages is at its greatest.

The Political Threat

The natural balance inherent in the first three laws of economics is readily seen. Unfortunately, the natural balance is at the mercy of gunslingers. Greed overrides need when armed by law and the unintended consequence of political interference with the natural balance is a long fall toward economic and political destruction. The finest wealth creating system imaginable is lost. The gold standard is lost. Inflation begins. Unemployment begins. Unconscionable wage gaps flower. And the legacy of a middle class disappears.

Contents

About the Author

G. Peter Trygstad, PE, BSEE, is an electrical engineer licensed as a professional engineer in the State of Washington. He worked for the Naval Undersea Warfare Center, Division Keyport, for three decades participating in development of underwater weapon systems. His present interest is the economics of freedom and free enterprise.

About the Book

The Federal Reserve bashed the American economy in the year 2000 because investments in the private stock market were paying much more than investments in federal debt (bills, notes, and bonds) at maturity. Their colossal alibi was to slow an 'overheating' economy. But their real purpose was to cripple the stock market and avoid a default of the national debt.

Many political lies bury rational economic thought today. Economies do not overheat. Progressive taxes on personal income are forwarded to consumers by changes in supply and demand. Social security taxes are not shared by employers (labor costs pass to the market). Labor unions gain buying power by pushing minimum wage labor down (the national wage is finite). And monopolies always require political support. That is real economics. And this information, while absolutely true, is not government approved.

A natural economy is superbly controlled by supply and demand. But career seeking politicians create inflation, stagflation, wage gaps, recession, and depression in their gross economic ignorance and self centered pursuit of campaign contributions.

The author explains the economic interactions between private enterprise and political force. The political solution is a return to Laissez Faire. But can politicians arrive at economic truths before economic disaster befalls the nation? The depression Congress could not. And the new Congress is their clone.

Warning

Once you understand this manuscript, you will not be able to read a newspaper or view the evening news without recognizing a political lie and, before long, identifying the chronic political liars.

Part i.

Prelude to a Tyranny

There was a time when the author thought that a majority might amiably reach agreement on issues of taxing and spending if they possessed a common knowledge and a common integrity. But knowledge is certainly not common and, apparently, neither is integrity.

The founders knew that those carrying the burden of taxes must be those who are receiving the benefits. They made it a Constitutional imperative. Unfortunately the Supreme Court ignores their imperative. The common bonds between men who earn in proportion to effort get corrupted by the political will and greed of those pursuing entitlements by force of law. And if integrity is not a possession of the majority, a democracy could initiate a return trip to our feral ancestry and a vicious future. Part I introduces our political landscape.

Chapter 1

The Political Landscape

All civilized men share a common dictum. Thou shall not steal. This paramount rule of civilized men does not exist in the animal world. Many animal species exist in pecking orders. The pecking order is established by force. Civilized men have tried to replace force with cooperation. They engage in free enterprise. Every day people will enter into agreements and trade. Both parties to a trade walk away from the exchange happier for their encounter. Each party has gained something which he alone cannot or chooses not to provide for himself. It is a pleasant exchange.

Enter the element of force. No mutual agreement can be reached unless both parties to an agreement **gain**. But if an unearned gain is seized by one party, the other party loses. And losing must be imposed by force.

Theft involves the armed thug acting as an individual or as a member of a gang. Seizure involves agents armed by authority of law. In either event someone is losing by law or outlaw.

Some of the various names for theft are listed below.

- Robbery is the theft of ones income or property by force or threat.
- Fraud is theft by guile instead of by gun.
- Perjury is the breaking of any oath or formal promise.
- Extortion is theft of money by threat or misuse of authority.
- Embezzlement is the theft of funds held in trust.

Your government engages in all of the listed offenses big time. Of course the politicians will deny their participation in acts of thievery. And they create political euphemisms for concealing their participation in theft from taxpayers or consumers. Some of those follow.

- Campaign Financing
- Collective Bargaining
- Overheating Economy
- Monetary Policy

- Deficit Spending
- Anti Trust
- Economic Bailouts

Finally let us look at the political euphemisms that government has coughed up for the unique **economic disasters** that arise from Congressional creation of national debt, counterfeiting of the money supply, and the legalized pilfering of the natural economy.

- Inflation
- Stagflation
- Wage Gaps
- Recession
- Depression

Why these unintended consequences continually occur (they are not limited to America) is readily understood when the political motives for their creation are illuminated. But the political motives for government behavior are not pretty. In our country it is largely Congressmen seeking careers in the House of Bribes. And it is pretty much the same at state level or anywhere else.

All crimes are variations of theft. Government employs all kinds of misleading euphemisms for seizing the wealth of others and redistributing it to those who have not earned it and have no honest title to it.

In sharp contrast to the gun slingers, civilized people embrace a code,

Thou shall not steal.

This is the code of civilization. This signature decree does not appear in the animal kingdom. And in the human race this signature decree is not embraced by those residing on the political left. Among these troglodytes the new political euphemism for concealing their theft is,

Redistribution

Socialists and progressives hold the liberal attitude that some (the more capable) owe others (meaning the less capable or the indolent) a living. Karl Marx, the father of socialism, espoused the socialist creed.

**"From each in accordance with his ability,
to each in accordance with his need."**

The creed seems to end on a note of benevolence, dear reader. But let us not forget it starts on a note of animosity toward and enslavement for, those with ability. The egregious nature of the socialist creed is clarified by reversing the phrasing and ending on its note of animosity.

"Some shall pull themselves up by pulling others down."

The words are not as pretty now, dear reader. But they are not unfamiliar. Animal life is organized to survive without intellect. They survive by organizing in a pecking order. The alpha animal rises by pulling another down. Karl Marx was just another naked ape exhibiting his ancestral behavior. And so are his socialist followers.

Now one may view the true nature of socialism. The socialist creed justifies theft and redistribution. But theft on a grand scale requires government participation on a grand scale to quell violence and prevent retribution. The civil society will not tolerate theft. A socialist society will practice it at an enormous cost.

Affluence will flower in abundance in the society that outlaws theft under any guise. Affluence is gained without force when one must gain the cooperation of others by offering them something in return. In free enterprise people pull themselves up by pulling up others in an exchange of labor for the products of labor. Cooperation happily replaces coercion and malice where coercion is outlawed.

Cooperation and affluence are hallmarks of free enterprise and a free people.

The socialist moron cannot embrace the concept that one gains wealth by pulling up others in a free society. That is how it is done among the free. The socialist will embrace the use of government force for pulling down others and advancing himself. But he and his society are losers.

Forgive me for introducing the socialist as a moron. But the socialist is a predator. Those with earning power are his prey. Greed is his motive. Altruism is his alibi. Zero is his economic IQ. What should he be called?

Many people believe that Marx's creed represents compassion. It does not. It represents servitude. One can well imagine the slave owner of the antebellum South muttering the same benevolent (and self serving) creed over his slaves,

**"From each in accordance with his ability,
to each in accordance with his need"**

The clones of Simon Legree reside in socialist government today. The new slave owners think that taxpayers exist for the benefit of government.

John F. Kennedy admonished Americans to serve their country. Note how he confuses country with government, and servitude with gratitude,

**"Ask not what your country can do for you,
ask what you can do for your country."**

Liberals make no distinction between country (which is your culture and your language) and government (which can be your servant or your master). Bill Clinton said that one cannot love his country and hate his government. The Third Reich held the same belief.

Countering their love for government, the founders believed that the purpose of government was to secure the unalienable rights of men and to defend them from the greed of other men. But individual rights cannot exist in a pecking order, not in anthropology nor in political ideology.

The founders and the socialist left have diametrically opposed points of view. The founders wisely distrusted government power. The political left sees government as a benevolent master and the people as mere servants requiring government direction. The leftists want people to believe that those whose greed is armed by law are more generous and caring than are free men pursuing mutual benefit in unarmed free enterprise.

People that believe in limited government call themselves republicans. Others may call themselves libertarians. On the other hand people who believe that the masses (their term) are too ignorant to take responsibility for their lives and that political voices must prevail call themselves democrats or liberals. They do not ask if the people deliver a superior economic performance without government direction than with government direction. And they would not like the answer.

Former president Bill Clinton is a quintessential example of the political left. In a speech before business people in Buffalo, NY, on 20 January 1999, Clinton declared that American taxpayers should not be given a tax break because they cannot be trusted to spend their money right. His exact stutter was reported in the news,

"We could give it all back to you and hope you spend it right. But I think. Here is the problem. If you don't spend it right…"

Free men gain through personal integrity and private contract. Armed and arrogant men gain through force. Members of the gain by force camp include liberals, progressives, and environmentalists. These people do not trust free men and appear incapable of economic reasoning. They will not leave other men alone.

The nature of the struggle between the political right and the political left in politics is that of a struggle between civil men who disclaim the use of force in free enterprise and arrogant men who will use the force of government for imposing economic redistribution. At least that is their alibi. But that too is highly questionable.

The leftist will never ask if the natural distribution of wealth in accordance with ability and effort is superior to a government distribution of wealth in accordance with ignorance, indolence, and greed (greed overrides need when armed by law). The leftist will assault ability and effort, destroy freedom and free enterprise, and expand human poverty through his vicious pursuit of the earnings of others. His animal behavior is not apparent to him. Nor can he recognize the destruction of wealth in his wake.

But civil men respect free men and their ability to earn. They recognize civilization itself as a product of free men, free enterprise, and a five thousand year old creed.

Thou shall not steal.

Chapter 2

Collectivism

Most of us have heard the expression **honor among thieves**. What is alluded to is the fact that even thieves in a gang will not steal from each other. They could not do so and maintain their cohesiveness as a group. Cooperation is required for collective action and an unwritten code to respect each others person and property is assumed within the group.

Ironically, while some may honor a code of civilized behavior within their collective, they will organize to take by force or force of law the wealth of others outside of their collective. They advance by pulling down others.

Collectivism is embraced by tenants in landlord tenant legislation or in rent control. It is embraced by women in women's rights groups. It is embraced by racists in racial legislation. It is embraced by homosexuals in pursuit of license for their behavior and of entitlements for the health consequences. It is embraced by labor unions in coercing wages above market by threatening corporations with huge losses in a strike and intimidating competitive labor at the picket line. It is embraced by the legal monopoly in pursuit of class action lawsuits and exorbitant fees and fines.

Collectivism is embraced by zealots of all sorts, and politicians everywhere are on their shopping lists.

But collectivism is thwarted at political boundaries. Religious sects, industries, corporations, doctors, entrepreneurs, retirees, and others can elude the tyrannical heel of collectivist government by leaving its jurisdiction. But there are those who would leave no escape.

Walter Cronkite, favored world government.[1] Many liberals view political coercion as a means to unite the world in peace. But government is an instrument of force. And unrestrained force promotes enmity.

---

[1] Walter Cronkite, "A Reporter's Life," Alfred A. Knopf, New York 1996, p. 128.

Coercing the world into one government will guarantee nothing. The United States engaged in a war between the states in 1861. Coercion is not the answer.

Free enterprise, free people, and governments of limited power are the answer. The founders knew that. We have strayed far. And we pay for it.

The UN is a collective of political tyrannies. They are eager to redistribute the wealth of the world from those who possess it to those who have not allowed its creation. Their governments have not provided the legal environment or the political integrity for private wealth to grow. People do not build where the fruits of their labor are seized by law or outlaw.

Socialists will not embrace a philosophy of honesty and effort for creating an abundance of wealth. Instead they embrace the ideology of enslaving the capable with the guns of government.

The world's problem is to find a means to promote free enterprise and the private sector and to contain the growth of the gun slinging political sector. As always, greed overrides need when armed by law. We must allow private cooperation and constrain public coercion.

The founders believed that individual rights were imperative to the pursuit of happiness. It is the individual that produces the wealth. It is the individual that pays the taxes. It is the individual that dies for his country. Collective rights arise from individuals in the collective. They do not exist on their own, not among a free people.

But a democracy can not represent the individual. It can only represent a collective. And that puts individual rights in great danger. In the larger political landscape democracy is used by those who would subject private decisions to a public vote and to seize and redistribute the earnings of a minority.

> **The powers not delegated to the United States by the Constitution, nor prohibited by it to the States, are reserved to the States respectively, or to the people.**

The Tenth Amendment is a restraining order on federal authority. It illuminates the enumerated powers doctrine. It reserves powers not delegated to the

Congress in Section 8 to the people of the states. But liberal justices will find new meaning in the Constitution. They take political power from the people and arrogate it to the Congress, unelected federal agencies, and organized labor.

Government does not grow by pleasing its paying customers as private enterprise is constrained to do. First it grows by ignoring constitutional constraints and interfering with private enterprise. Here government initiates gross economic problems by its political interference with supply and demand. Then it seizes yet more powers to ameliorate the economic destruction and implement damage control. The economic damage is never anticipated nor understood by the economic zeroes causing it. That is why government must be chained with Constitutional restraints.

Individuals can suffer economic problems by their own misbehavior, but government can spread economic problems border to border and beyond.

Great civilizations in the past were brought down by class warfare between taxpayers and tax beneficiaries. First a government expands, eventually it impoverishes its taxpayers, and then it finds itself economically unable to carry its beneficiaries or defend its borders. And they never seem to comprehend the economics of their fall!

Democracy may show that the human race is not ready to sustain civilization with participatory government. There may simply be too many predators in our midst.

The threat comes from collectives organized for economic gain at the expense of others and a Congress that returns collectivist legislation for the necessary campaign funding.

The threat comes from those that see themselves as government beneficiaries and government growth as wonderful and benign. But government growth is not benign. It is cancerous. And it is deadly. It does not quit growing until its host dies.

Chapter 3

Dirty Laundry

The disastrous twentieth century that Americans endured was caused by politicians seeking Congressional careers at any public cost. The United States Congress created one economic disaster after another in their endless search for campaign funds. It has not ended.

It takes money, more money than most can earn honestly, to get elected to public office at federal or state level. Bill Gates and a few other entrepreneurs may earn enough from honest enterprise to qualify as an exception. But as we shall see, honest money is denigrated by the leftist American news media. Leftists seem to view the wealthy as the source of all economic problems. They cannot see themselves in that role.

Some CEO's of large corporations might afford the 800 million price tag of a presidential bid or a 50 million price tag of a seat in the Senate, but why would they? It is, after all, just an installment payment.

The price of a seat must be met again and again, term after term. Nine of ten congressional incumbents are returned to office election after election. Their salaries cannot approach the amount required for their reelection. Where do incumbents find all that loot?

They find it from their marriage with campaign contributors.

Congressional seats are basically for sale. Special interests buy them. Incumbents sell them. Congressmen work for contributions. If the incumbent fails to represent his campaign contributors by failing to promote their legislative agenda, he will face reelection without their funds. Consequently they represent their campaign fund sources.

Their Constitutional duty is to represent the taxpayer. But damn few will or can.

Only the wealthy can compete for election to office without accepting special interest funds and returning special interest legislation. But are

Congressmen accepting bribes? Not by their definition. And theirs is the only one that counts. They are accepting campaign contributions.

The Constitution calls for the removal from office of all civil officers impeached and convicted of bribery. But it rarely happens. A bit of discretion is all that is required. Any bribe can be accepted under the euphemism of a political contribution.

The campaign reform acts allow politicians to accept special interest money within limits. The emphasis is on limits rather than on acceptance. Since bribes are hardly distinguishable from contributions, political contributions are laundered into legality. This is dirty laundry.

Because of political contributions, your federal government is corrupt. Your state government is also. So is your city government.

In 1992 Ross Perot spent fifty seven million of his own money for a White House bid. The media loved his money but withheld its support.

In November 1994, Michael Huffington used 29 million of personal funds to campaign for a Senate seat from California. He was roasted by the news media for attempting to buy a seat. In 1996 it was Phil Gramm who was roasted for financing himself. And in 2000, the leftist media was whining about Steve Forbes. He was trying to buy the White house.

The sad but cold fact is that elections are normally bought by candidates. Their election is purchased with campaign funds. No funds, no seat!

Many people have noted the hate toward the wealthy apparent in the liberal news media. Only those who must seek the contributions of special interests are allowed to compete without ridicule.

But why does the leftist news media create a scandal over honest money and favor laundered money? They have a political agenda to enact!

Honest money can buy only seats. Laundered money buys legislation.

In 1988 Booth Gardner ran for governor of the state of Washington. The Washington State Employees Union and the Washington Education Association contributed roughly 90 thousand dollars to Booth's election campaign.

Booth prevailed. The governor and the state legislature then routed a 385 million dollar tax surplus to the labor unions in pay raises and in school funding. Taxpayers were slammed.

The two unions received 4000 dollars for every dollar invested in the Booth campaign. Some call this quid pro quo.

The same game with different faces was repeated in 1996 and in 2004.

The labor union cannot be unaware that their collective's generous income is not freely provided by market demand. It was seized from taxpayers and redistributed by authority of government. And the greatest of all political lies was deployed to quench any criticism,

It's for the Kids!

In November of 2008, Senator Obama gained the White House with the help of an estimated 800 million dollars in campaign contributions. Contributors to his campaign may demand a trillion (1000 billion) dollar return on their investment.

Immediately following the election, the Speaker of the House, Nancy Pelosi, was demanding hundreds of billions in tax revenue for bailing out automakers hammered by overpriced labor and for bailing out lending institutions hammered by Congressional edicts to lend to losers. She intends to transfer huge amounts of tax revenue from low paid labor to highly paid labor. Some call this damage control. Others call it insane. But the Congress initiated the damage. And the taxpayers receive the punishment!

The founders would surely view the acceptance of campaign funds as a potential bribe and the delivery of the sought legislation as proof of purchase. But today it is merely campaign finance. The political prohibition of bribery has been nullified by legality.

Not all interest groups are formed for purposes of pulling someone else down. Some form because they are the targets of government theft. Thus there are two classes of interest groups. There are collectives who are targeted (the prey) and collectives favored for redistribution of the loot (the predators).

Some targets of the political left are the tobacco industry, the chemical industry, the oil industry, the nuclear power industry, the medical profession, corporations and entrepreneurs. The leftoids see these collectives as lucrative sources for looting. The legal industry, the welfare industry, the Indian tribes, and labor unions are the beneficiaries of run away litigation and taxation.

Wealth is a finite quantity. What government gives Paul, it seizes from Peter. Government is very good at creating income gaps between the politically favored and the politically disfavored and blaming the private sector for the gaps. And it is incapable of containing its own vicious appetite for more and more taxes.

Greed overrides need when armed by law.

Chapter 4

Force

Government is an instrument of force. Look around the political world. Notice those wearing the guns and the badges of authority. Notice those that are licensed to kill. Observe armed groups killing each other. One group is the government. The other group wants to govern. The salient characteristic of government anywhere is deadly force.

Contrast government with free enterprise. The salient characteristic of free enterprise, wherever people are free, is voluntary cooperation. Food and shelter are produced. All subsistence needs are created. And in a free society, where the fruits of your labor are protected by law, affluence is created. If your society is free, there is no role for force except to defend your rights, your property, and your life. Put the emphasis on **defend**.

Civilized men defend themselves from uncivil men by creating government. But the never ending problem is one of keeping the guns of government out of the hands of thieves. In America the Constitution was written to call into existence and to limit the power of federal government. But the Constitution is unarmed and the political left will redefine its meaning from a restraining order into a license for tyranny. They hide their treason under the euphemism of a 'living constitution.'

The two enemies of the people are criminals and government, so let us tie the second down with the chains of the Constitution so that the second will not become the legalized version of the first.

--Thomas Jefferson--

Part ii.
The Players

The stage has been set and it is time to introduce the political players. The players often choose different names in different national landscapes but they can usually be placed by their party's philosophy on a political horizon that varies from rationalized theft on the political left to honesty and self reliance on the political right. Society is a mix of people from uncivil to civil. And people reveal their nature, or their ignorance, by their choice of politicians or political parties to represent them. Interestingly enough, the political progression from left to right also exhibits an age progression from youth to maturity. We become ladies and gentlemen as we get older and wiser. At least many of us do.

Chapter 5

The Profit Motive

Mother Nature or nature's god created the profit motive to guide natural evolution and ultimately the evolution of civilization. Socialists hate the entrepreneur society and the profit motive. They are blind to the benefits that entrepreneurs distribute into the landscape. And they envy what entrepreneurs gain for themselves.

In December of 1991 an event occurred that is unique in the annals of human history. A world power abruptly ceased its political existence. There was no civil war. There was no invasion. There were no conquering armies. The disintegration was unique. The bonds of the political union dissolved spontaneously.

The union was held together by the bonds of socialism and the marriage had utterly failed its expectations. The union was that of several Soviet Socialist Republics. It was time for a divorce.

Could they have recognized their failures, if private enterprise in the West had not illuminated the difference? Would they instead have viewed human population as exceeding natural resources and engaged in genocide? Some environmental zealots embrace the idea. And they embrace solutions to imagined problems that are inhuman in their ramifications. Consider what the Soviets did to their people in the pursuit of ideological zealotry. Stalin murdered more of his people than did the Nazis.

The Soviets interfered with the natural economic laws of supply and demand. The Soviets had tasked their government to do the impossible. They had tasked their bureaucracy to direct their economy at command level. But economic direction normally comes from the bottom up. Supply and demand represents the aggregate behavior of millions of buyers and sellers at the grass roots level.

The Soviets directed their economy from the top down and feedback from the end user could be unwelcome. Their upside down economic model had no chance of performing with the efficiency and balance of a free people engaging in free enterprise. Government by its very nature can only impede a free and natural economy with wholly unnecessary legal constraints.

How many thousands of bureaucrats does it take to allow an economy to thrive? Can socialists not link affluence with free people and private enterprise?

The U was was R was an example of trying to accomplish with political force that which is superbly done by free men acting through cooperation and mutual benefit. But the Soviets were not alone. American economic disasters serve also as examples of political interference in a natural economy.

The Soviet Socialists regressed from private enterprise to state enterprise. They regressed from individual rights to state rights. They regressed from profit driven individual effort to threat driven collective effort. They adopted the means of survival of the tribe. They abandoned free enterprise and chose the economics of scarcity.

Consumer shortages in the U wait wait R were expressed by long waiting lines or waiting lists. Waiting substituted for rationing. Rationing would embarrass the utopian state. But rationing is the very function of pricing. Prices balance supply with demand. And shortages or surpluses are avoided.

But the greatest insult to nature was the Soviet assault on the profit motive. Generations before Lenin a young predator, Karl Marx, looked over his economic landscape and saw inequities. Some people were wealthy, some were not. In particular he was not. The fact that private wealth was naturally distributed in accordance with ability and years of effort meant nothing to the socialist. Like royalty, he should have wealth by entitlement. Marx faulted free enterprise.

Industry was rising. Entrepreneurs were gaining wealth. But Karl believed that entrepreneurs were hogging the fruits of labor. This is a common affliction.

But it is not true. Private enterprise creates wealth in accordance with ability and distributes it in accordance with ability. But an abundance of wealth arises from that very incentive. There is no better way to create abundance.

All over the Earth, animals are born and raised. Then they are released into the landscape. Parental care, superb while it lasts, is withdrawn. The young are trained to survive and then they are released to survive on their own. Were it not so, the young would live at the expense of the old. When the old passed on, so would the species. Self reliance is the way nature sustains life on Earth.

This was the way of men until socialists arose and decided that cradle to grave care should be an entitlement. The natural human family was not caring enough. Some were dysfunctional. A government tyranny could embrace us all.

The state shall raise humans. Socialists never add the qualifier, until they cost too much. Then the state after taking from them their freedom to care for themselves, will abandon them in their twilight hour.

But socialism is of a sudden superior to nature. Never mind that Mother Nature, without central planning, was able to develop over the ages an Earth teeming with life. Never mind that Mother Nature created a natural economy whose superb functioning few can understand and appreciate. And never mind that all life that arose over the passage of time was driven by a natural profit motive.

There is no better explanation for the compelling urge that drives evolution and makes all life possible, than that of a profit motive. Nothing is done by living nature except to profit. The bird does not fly except to profit. The cat does not hunt except to profit. The flower does not turn to follow the path of the sun across the sky except to profit. The leaves will also. Long before men learned to count and invented money to keep score, the profit motive was there.

The profit motive tells us and other creatures of nature that we are doing things right. <u>Profit is nature's feedback mechanism.</u> If we profit, we continue our behavior. If we fail, we change it. We live. We learn.

Along comes Marx. He turns nature on her ear. Profit should be separated from effort. Effect shall be separated from cause. Some should profit from the efforts of others. Loot the producers and redistribute the profits.

They pretend to pay us and we pretend to work.

That was the saying of the unhappy workers behind the iron curtain. Their incentive to improve their condition was stilled by state slavery. In the U was was R, there was no profit in effort. Affluence is built by effort. And effort is in proportion to profit.

One can motivate a slave to work by threatening him with harm. He will not risk his life. But much more effort can be enticed from a man by luring him with profit instead of pushing him with a threat. People will take risks for profit. That is why free people prosper while socialism destroys the work ethic of societies held in state slavery.

Free enterprise is remarkably honest where government influence has corrupted it least. The reason is the profit motive. Theft in house harms the corporation's competitiveness in the market place. A lack of work ethic harms the corporation. Feather bedding harms the corporation. The profit motive demands civilized behavior within the organization and in its customer relations. The more civilized the behavior, the more competitive is the corporation and the better it is for the consumer. And, until recently, top heavy corporations faced 'hostile' takeovers when management seized excess profits and drove down the company stock (but corrupt government saved them).

In addition the profit motive promotes efficiency. Private enterprise is self correcting and innovative under good management. Under bad management it fails in the competitive market place and departs the landscape. Like Enron.

The reader may now realize that the profit motive, besides driving evolution, is in this epoch driving mankind toward civil conduct and civilization. Free enterprise is forcing human cooperation on a grand scale.

But the profit motive is finely directed by loss. Losses can not be sustained in free enterprise. Losses cut unprofitable ventures forcing a free society into productive pathways. The salient characteristic of an affluent society is maximum freedom and minimum government.

Conversely and unfortunately, losses never constrain government. Losses expand government. When government experiences losses it will not quit its misfeasance. Taxes are simply raised and the losses sustained. And government, unlike Enron, never departs the landscape.

The federal government is fighting losing wars on drugs, poverty, transportation, energy production, environmental demons, and terror. But only the private sector feels the losses.

These wars cannot be won. Only a prosperous and free private sector can remove or minimize the alleged threats. By limiting taxing and spending, government is forced to behave like free enterprise and a free people. It is forced to use its income in an efficient and prudent manner just as members of a civil society must. It is forced into change for the better.

The political left wants no limit on taxing power. More revenue is always needed. Of course it is! As taxes remove money from productivity in the private sector, national output falls, the dollar loses buying power, and tax revenues do also. There is a natural limit to taxing. The economist, Arthur B. Laffer, noted the phenomena many years ago. Yet some leftist economists (including a Nobel Prize winner) think that government bailouts and labor unions can fix economic problems. Actually they create and sustain them.

When your government is handcuffed by expenditure limits, when it has the same spending constraints that free enterprise experiences, it will spend taxpayer's money prudently and wisely. It will limit waste. It will punish theft. It will seek out and destroy bureaucratic deadwood and rescind its enactment. Nature's wonderful profit motive will guide it there.

Chapter 6

The Nature of the Liberal Left

Human beings have two inheritances. One is their genetic or biological heritage. The other is their civil heritage. They are often in conflict. What you are genetically is fixed at conception. What you are civilly is within human control. Those who exercise little or no self control behave like animals and often, live like animals.

Animals and some men live in a pecking order. This is an enforced order where the alphas prevail and others are prevailed over. Uncivil men who rule by force live here. There is no justice in a pecking order and there is no guilt. Justice is a civil concept and guilt can only be felt by men of conscience. Civil men recognize a responsibility to behave as they would have others behave towards them. A pecking order does not.

Civil men respect private property and do not steal. Respect for another's property and the prohibition of theft are inseparable. One cannot exist without the other. Honesty is a civil concept. Honesty is not embraced by animals and socialists. Socialists will justify theft. They appear to be the inhabitants of an unconscious pecking order.

People who can tolerate the enslavement of those with ability are also well capable of lying. A lack of integrity does not allow one fault while excluding another. Civil men do not steal and have little need for lies. Uncivil men engage in theft and have a great need for lies.

Civil men restrain their animal impulses. Uncivil men don't. Human problems begin at puberty. The body is ready for adulthood but the mind is not. Restraint must be accepted on faith by the young. It is the gift of a civil society. Our feral instincts must be civilly directed or personal tragedies result. Only primitives, liberals, and public schools grant adolescents a sex life at puberty.

Human experience and knowledge gets passed from generation to generation by fathers to sons, by mothers to daughters, and by mentors and written languages. Universities, libraries, and other institutes of men are repositories of knowledge. Human knowledge cannot be passed genetically. Knowledge must be gained by heritage.

Human experience and knowledge culminate in wisdom. Wisdom is the burden of elders. It is a burden the young must first learn and then conserve if civilization is to survive and advance. Most men embrace conservative philosophy as they grow older and wiser. They continue to learn.

On the other hand the young and dumb largely embrace liberalism. It is not amazing that some of the young arrive on the university campus prepared to disseminate political wisdom rather than absorb collected knowledge. Many believe the campus is the kingdom of intellectuals and the outer world is the realm of dummies. The campus elite will organize political demonstrations and engage in riotous behavior.

And the dummies in the leftist news media are there to report and to spread student wisdom to the reluctant taxpayers out there in dummy land. But the university cannot impart wisdom, it cannot impart intellect, it can only impart knowledge.

Sir James Mathew Barrie expressed his view of the arrogant young thusly,

"I am not young enough to know everything."

Being young and dumb does not mean a lack of intellect. It means a lack of experience and a lack of knowledge. We have all been there.

Unfortunately, many liberals think that the fruits of labor should be shared just like sunshine and rain. Their philosophy does not respect private property or the efforts of others to earn their share of the wealth. They are entitled to wealth because they share the landscape. They possess the arrogance of kings.

The liberal left will invariably demand better treatment for the tax beneficiary and the criminal. But they have no conscience for the taxpayer or the victims of crime. One cannot embrace both the predator and his prey. In politics as in logic it is a mutually exclusive relation. One must support one or the other. Liberals reveal the nature of the political left in their tolerance of predators.

Liberals reveal their nature in politics. They are not prepared to leave others alone. They must prevail over those who lack their confidence in the nanny state. They are prepared to use government in any way possible.

Elbridge Gerry was a governor of Massachusetts. His party in the legislature redrew the boundary lines of Essex County to pack the opposition party into one district allowing his party to prevail in others (1812). The outline of the created district looked like a salamander. The press came to calling it a Gerrymander. One might think that rigging an election by boundary tampering was illegal. But it isn't.

The Supreme Court (circa 1989) let stand an appeals court decision which had rejected a Republican challenge to gerrymandering in California. The liberal lower court (the infamous ninth circuit) said that gerrymandering is not unconstitutional unless the other party is excluded from the political process as a whole (try to find that in the Constitution). Republicans had elected a California governor, a United States Senator, and 17 of 45 House members.[2]

Note the stutter step danced by the liberal court. Gerrymandering cannot affect elections for governor or the U.S. Senate. State boundaries cannot be moved by politicians practicing election rigging. State wide elections were never the issue, but they were included in the alibi of the court.

What clearer indication of the nature of the liberal left does one need? And didn't the court reveal an argument against their own decision in their search for an alibi?

If Republicans prevailed in statewide elections, we must presume an honest election would result in Republicans prevailing in the House. But they don't (17 of 45). They are not even close.

Those that cast the votes decide nothing.
Those who count the votes decide everything.

--Joseph Stalin--

And now we can define a basic difference between liberalism and conservatism. Our liberalism has its roots in our genetic or animal inheritance. Our conservatism derives from our cultural inheritance, our civilization. This too is the political horizon. There exists a natural distribution of people from liberal left to conservative right. It is a distribution from primitive behavior and rationalized theft on the political left to civil behavior and the prohibition of theft on the political right. It is a distribution from collective theft to personal honesty and integrity. And it is a distribution from younger to older and wiser.

The founders set 25 years of age for membership in the House and 30 years of age for membership in the Senate in 1789. Shouldn't their electors be 25 and 30 years of age respectively? Shouldn't they also be older and wiser?

The political left will always be found behind attempts to lower the voting age or to allow felons to vote. The politicians know that the young are

---

[2] Cited under Editorials, Boosts for Gerrymandering, The Sun, 21 February 89, pg. A10.

politically ignorant. And they know that felons lack integrity. But do they think that the young or the felonious improve the electorate?

Or do the predators, who inhabit the political left, know their roots? Do they see the young as gullible and felons as allies to enlist in their penchant for taking earned wealth from others?

Human nature improves as we examine the political spectrum from left to right and from younger to older. Our primitive ancestry seems to wear off with intellectual growth and a civil nature assumes its place.

Chapter 7

The Political Spectrum

The predatory nature of the political left has been introduced without the weight of proof. The weight of proof is found in the damages they have inflicted on formerly free economies wherever they gain political power. The common thread among leftists around the world is their pursuit of wealth by employing the guns of government. Free enterprise in contrast employs only agreement and contract in the pursuit of wealth.

Free enterprise is the economic behavior of a free people. The term private enterprise will often be used instead of the term free enterprise in this manuscript because so little economic freedom remains in America. And as to defining a political spectrum, anyone may do that.

When George Wallace ran for the presidency on a third party ticket in 1968, he claimed that there wasn't a dimes worth of difference between Democrats and Republicans. He was wrong. There isn't a dimes worth of difference between Democrats and socialists. But it suited George's campaign. The Libertarians make a similar claim today.

The Libertarians have added a vertical axis to the political horizon. It progresses from authoritarian to libertarian. In this manner they can place the two major political parties in one camp, authoritarian. They say Democrats are economically authoritarian and Republicans are morally authoritarian. True enough, but the political left is an absolute threat to freedom and prosperity.

Democrats support women's rights, gay rights, minority rights, animal rights, tenant rights, and myriads of other collective rights without regard as to how these narrowly defined rights clash with classical individual rights. Collective rights always target others for theft. Thus collectivists do not seek rights. They seek entitlements. Ironically, the political left will exclude sexual behavior from their long list of behaviors requiring government correction.

But the political right wont. Conservatives will attempt to civilize the moral landscape with prohibitions. Thus the stage is set for confrontations. But unbridled use of the gun to promote either economic equality or moral behavior divides society.

What conservatives need to learn is that morality expands as impositions on others are curbed by individual rights and freedom. What liberals need to learn is that free enterprise creates wealth in accordance with ability and effort and it distributes wealth in the same manner. But the distribution provides the incentive and an affluent society is the result.

The political spectrum spans the political horizon from those who seek unearned entitlements on the left to those who seek to keep their earnings on the right. Those on the political right believe in self reliance. The state can only insure their rights. Those in need can be helped by family first and charity next. The assumption here is that the family remains the principle unit of social life and that it will not be destroyed by political greed and envy.

Those on the political left believe in state reliance. Taxpayers exist for the betterment of society. And in particular they exist for their benefit.

Honesty and integrity are not properties of the human animal, nor are they possessed by the criminal. They are acquired by heritage. They are the precepts of civilized men and civilization. And they are missing among those inhabiting the political left.

Chapter 8

The Democrats

This book is about the political destruction of a natural economy over a century by politicians seeking careers in the United States Congress. Two political parties are the principle players.

As the twentieth century progressed, the political left came to dominate the Democratic political party. The political center joined the political right in the Republican political party.

The Democratic political party today views government as a means to redistribute wealth rather than as a means to secure the rights of the individual. They view tax cuts as government losses rather than economic gains by a free people. They must do so. Democratic incumbents have a political symbiosis with tax beneficiaries. Their power is built on the backs of taxpayers.

Point two of the Communist Manifesto demands **a heavy progressive or graduated income tax.** Democrats promote the tax under an alibi of fairness. Its real purpose is to maximize tax revenue. And it does that in a way that few citizens could have imagined. Inelastic market demand can shift income taxes from targeted individuals to consumers. But a graduated tax appears to harness the capable and profiting from the efforts of others is the socialist dream.

Any society will harbor a percentage of freeloaders.[3] The political left seeks to enslave the labor of those with ability. But redistribution diverts wages from the hands of productive people. Still the leftist party continues its ignorant economic assault on affluence.

A huge special interest of the Democratic Party in America is the millions of unwed mothers and their live in boyfriends on welfare. They enjoy income and numerous benefits that are not taxable and they deliver their votes to Democrats. They deliver their burdens to taxpayers.

---

[3] Economists call those who do not contribute free riders. I call them freeloaders. I am an engineer.

Marxist labor unions and Democrats have long been symbionts. Unions fund political election kitties and politicians permit unions to coerce wages many times above market value. But higher wages here are compensated by minimum wages or no wages over there. The symbionts create huge wage gaps and chronic unemployment.

Another major funding source for the Democratic Party is the environmental zealot. The zealot is a single minded individual often without credentials in the field in which he pontificates. Zealots can impoverish society through green taxes and the decimation of nuclear and fossil energy sources. They could restore a primitive landscape and with it a short life span.

In 2002 the Association of Trial Lawyers of America became the largest single contributor to federal candidates. Nearly all recipients are Democrats. In 2004 a trial lawyer, a man who seized millions of dollars from insurance companies by suing maternity doctors, was the parties vice presidential candidate.

Finally there is the left leaning news media in America. The media outlets reside under many layers of taxation and political destruction in ringworm cities. The need for urban renewal is not seen as a result of regulation, litigation, and taxation. It is seen as a need for more of the same. Most news networks and big city newspapers support the leftist agenda. All political views insensitive to their self inflicted wounds will be labeled religious right, far right, or conservative. The media (with some notable exceptions) reveals itself in many ways as a voice of the political left.

This Democratic Party is an incredible array of special interests with taxing and redistributing in their hearts and with national news media as their mouths. Yet half of the electorate is not enlisting in their tax and spend philosophy. They recognize themselves as taxpayers and they recognize others as tax recipients. They are not blind.

Chapter 9

The Communist Manifesto
(1848)

Many members of the political left are socialists. They appear to steer its agenda. Let us visit the ten points of the Communist Manifesto for illustration.

Abolition of property in land and application of all rents of land to public purposes. In Washington State Referendum 48, a requirement to reimburse property owners for property rights taken by the state for environmental purposes was defeated by the Democratic Party and their toadies in the media.

A heavy progressive or graduated income tax. In 1913 the Congress enslaved a portion of American labor to the service of government. This tax is loved by the left. They believe that their economic targets will pay it. Some may, but most will not. Market forces will defeat its purpose.

Abolition of all rights of inheritance. In the fall of 1999 a Republican controlled Congress voted to abolish the estate and inheritance tax. Clinton vetoed the bill. Your kids cannot be trusted to spend their inheritance right.

Confiscation of the property of all immigrants and rebels. Confiscation! That is another government euphemism for legalized theft.

Centralization of credit in the hands of the state, by means of a national bank with State capital and an exclusive monopoly. The Federal Reserve controls the money supply, prints legal tender, and has a monopoly on money.

Centralization of the means of communication and transport in the hands of the state. Going there. Doing that. A work in progress.

Extension of factories and the instruments of production owned by the State; the bringing into cultivation of wastelands, and the improvement of the soil generally in accordance with a common plan. Democrats and environmentalists call this growth management or economic bailout. Socialists have always called it socialism.

Equal liability of all to labour. Establishment of industrial armies, especially for agriculture. Marx thought that unskilled labor was paramount in the production of wealth. He was wrong. Labor exists everywhere. Wealth does not.

Combination of agriculture with manufacturing industries; gradual abolition of the distinction between town and country, by a more equable distribution of the population over the country. Free enterprise, farming technology, freeways, and the private vehicle were taking us here. But leftoids today are screaming about urban sprawl. They want to stop taxpayer flight from ringworm jurisdictions. This point of the manifesto is the only point abandoned by Democrats. Free men cannot spend their money right.

Free education for all children in public schools. Abolition of children's factory labour in its present form. Combination of education with industrial production. Public schools have spread economic falsehoods, environmental falsehoods, and political falsehoods. When the hammer falls, the true cost of free education will be upon us.

One can see that Democrats and the political left have lots in common.

Chapter 10

The Republicans

Republicans are against the children. They are against the poor. They are against the little guy. And they are insensitive and mean spirited. This is the portrait of Republicans as painted by the leftist artists in the news media. But it is a bogus view.

Republicans are more likely to view free enterprise as the economic behavior of a free people. Many republicans recognize that limited governments preside over affluent economies and that tyrannies preside over third world economies.

Most Republicans believe in a republican form of government. A republican form of government is guaranteed to the states in Article. IV. Section. 4. of the Constitution. The individual is sovereign under a republican form of government. The state is to represent and serve the political will of the taxpayers.

Democrats, in general, embrace an opposite ideology. The will of the people must be harnessed to serve the state. The people cannot spend their money right. Only the state knows how to spend money.

Republicans believe in conserving the Constitution. Democrats, on the other hand, appoint judges that allow the Congress a free hand in expanding the domain of government. Article V of the Constitution provides the means for amendment thereof, requiring the participation and consent of three quarters of the states. But today five of nine judges (who ignore their oath to uphold the Constitution) can alter constitutional meaning. Liberals call the results of their tampering a living constitution.

The Constitution is a restraining order on federal expansion. Its purpose is to limit the interests of government. Democrats seek to expand those interests. The Constitution blocks their goals.

The Constitutional duty of the House of Representatives is to represent the taxpayer. The Republican party does it better than the other party can, but their backbone quivers under the constant accusations of Democrats that they are mean spirited and insensitive.

So the Democrats expand government by ignoring their duty to the taxpayer and courting tax beneficiaries. Republicans generally court the taxpayers. The Democrats think a simple majority is a license to seize taxes without consequence. They may not understand or care that rebellions are initiated by taxpayers.

But some may. Some Democrats seek to disarm the taxpayers under the ruse of keeping guns out of the hands of felons or children. But felons cannot be disarmed by legality. Neither can juvenile delinquents. Many members of the political left are afraid of armed taxpayers. They want taxpayers disarmed. They cannot admit to it. Few people understand the nature of the political assault on the second amendment today.

Republicans get most of the taxpayer's vote. People, who view the political left as predators organized for looting, are going to the Republican Party for protection.

As a result the major political parties are engaged in class warfare. Class warfare funds Congressional tenure.

Now we must talk of generalities. Men are taller than women. This is understood to be a generality. Someone who wants to refute the generality will espouse an exception. But exceptions are merely a tool of deception in politics and in the media. Liberal news sources will often use the exception for deception. Many environmentalists rely on deception.

Taken in general, most Republicans support the taxpayer. Republican voters are tax payers and Democratic voters are tax beneficiaries. And the liberal media expects you to believe that tax payers are selfish and that tax beneficiaries are their victims. Is this not the robber calling his reluctant victim selfish?

We must visit the political corruption of economics before the political landscape can be revealed in all its gory. The Democrats generally promote government as your benefactor and private enterprise as your nemesis. The Republicans generally view private enterprise with less suspicion and view government as the threat. Who are you to believe? You don't have to pick and choose. You can know.

Chapter 11

Political Deception

It is not illegal to lie. That is demonstrated in any election campaign. But one cannot call a liar a liar without risk. Politicians have made the rules. But the integrity of many on the political left is readily ascertained by comparing their political oratory with their voting record.

On June 6 of the year 2000 the House of Representatives passed the Death Tax Elimination Act. Clinton vetoed the bill. On a vote to override the veto on September 7, fourteen members of the House who originally supported the legislation switched their vote.[4]

A bill may be enacted with all yeas in the Congress. Although politically unlikely, the president could veto it. The Congress could then pass the bill on a vote to override the veto. The vote to override must find a two thirds majority in both chambers. The House had enough votes to override the veto on original passage of the act, but fell just fourteen votes shy on the vote to override. The bill died in the House.

Thirteen of fourteen representatives who changed their vote were Democrats. This is not a random distribution. Representatives may change their mind. But a thirteen to one imbalance across party lines reflects the lack of integrity of many who reside on the political left.

In another contest, a balanced budget amendment failed passage by one vote in the Senate. Seven Senators flip flopped on that vote. They all claimed they were for a balanced budget when running for their election. But then safely in office they voted against it. Six of the seven who changed their minds were Democrats.[5]

Again the distribution reflects a relative lack of integrity within the membership of the political left. Perjury is the breaking of any oath or formal promise. But politicians cannot be held to their promises.

A man that will rob Peter to pay Paul and then claim that he is Paul's benefactor is obviously lying (it was Peter) and engaging in theft to boot. But that is the nature of the political left. That is what they do. They use taxpayers to advance themselves. And they pretend to be generous and caring.

In a magnificent act of pretense, the Democrats proposed their own version of a balanced budget amendment that Republicans had to defeat. The bill was an artifice. Social Security was placed off budget. And as Social

---

[4] "Tax-Cut Turncoats Thwart Veto Override Votes," Dollars and Sense, National Taxpayers Union, Sep/Oct 2000, pg. 4.
[5] National Taxpayers Union letter to members dated 13 July 1995. pg. 2.

Security outlays approach one trillion annually, so too can deficit spending. Some balance!

Chapter 12

The Religious Right

We must introduce one more player in the political landscape. He plays the Achilles' heel of the Republican Party. He is the anti abortion zealot.

Five out of six potential pregnancies are prevented by American women practicing birth control.[6] These potential members of the human family were denied existence. This of course far exceeds the number of abortions that occur in the remaining one of six. One of four pregnancies is aborted. Thus abortions account for one fourth of one sixth or about four percent of birth control.

Let us face a simple if onerous fact. Birth control prevents babies from being born. It does not matter if intervention comes before or after conception. The end result is the same.

Miscarriages also prevent babies. Mother Nature has led the effort to thwart the flawed genome through miscarriage. And after eons, nature or nature's God has given men an ability to further that effort. We can choose to abort a developing genetic tragedy and opt for normal progeny at a later date. While some cannot accept choice, it represents a new beginning for others. Should others be denied their choice?

Most abortions are not sought because of genetic abnormalities, of course. It is not the genetic inheritance that is flawed. It is the civil inheritance that is flawed. That is why abortion is so important to the political left.

Whether by rape, incest, or human error, some pregnancies are not welcome. There has been no agreement to conceive. There is often no paternal support unless coerced by law. And there was no social contract.

---

[6] Judith Newman, "How Old is Too Old to have a Baby," Discover, April 2000, p. 65.

Having a child is an extremely important and long term personal commitment for a free individual. Put the emphasis on free.

The nature of the zealot is to force his beliefs on others. The Democratic political party normally welcomes zealots with their affinity to prevail by force of law and their campaign funds to influence the required legislation. But their party rejects the anti abortion zealot because abortions ameliorate licentious behavior. Damage control is the name of their game.

The Supreme Court noted that rights generally arise with birth. In one of few times that the court favored private decisions over political decisions, the court found abortion to be a privacy issue. In Roe vs. Wade the court essentially made abortion an issue between doctors and their patients unless there is a compelling state interest justifying state intervention.

The use of abortion for birth control is repulsive, but the political cost of prohibition is worse. In politics the losing interest faces a gun slinging government. Political decisions should be minimized and the economic and moral practices of men should be left in a more civil private sector.

The political left does not tolerate civil constraints on their behavior. But they do insist on enslaving the lives of others for their benefit. They gain much success in using the pro choice issue to cloak their political agenda which is decidedly no choice. They believe that a free people cannot distribute wealth fairly. But in their ignorance and greed, they have not allowed it.

Politics and economics are inseparably intertwined. They should not be. But one cannot understand economics today without illuminating the corrupting influence of politics. Natural economics has been distorted by law. We will begin the illumination next.

Part iii.

Economics

Economics explains how consumer demand interacts with market supply. Consumer demand is represented by all buyers and market supply is represented by all sellers. All sellers seek higher prices for their products or for their labor and all buyers seek lower prices for their purchases. These opposing forces will find their balance at prices to sell all products and wages to sell all labor if left undisturbed by government.

There can be no lingering shortage of products or surplus of labor in a free economy. In free enterprise consumers normally reside in a buyers market and labor normally resides in a sellers market. It could not be better. The relation is expressed in the first two laws of Economics in a Nutshell.

It takes the force of government to change a superb natural economic balance into an economic disaster of global proportions. Part III introduces natural economics and reveals its queering by corrupt and inept politicians.

Chapter 13

The Demand to Supply Ratio

Economic demand (in dollars) is represented by the sum of buyers seeking goods or services in the market. Economic supply is the sum of goods or services offered for sale. And the ratio of buyers (demand) to sellers (supply) has a fundamental influence on the pricing of their wares.

On a national scale the money supply limits prices. The sum of all prices cannot exceed the money in circulation. On a smaller scale prices may rise here and fall there. The demand in dollars is more elastic. And it is a change in local supply that will often dominate the demand to supply ratio.

There is more information in the demand to supply ratio than dollars per pound. Changes in the ratio predict whether prices will increase or decrease. Neither demand nor supply by itself can do this.

In the ratio (D/S) the numerator is demand and the denominator is supply. If the demand to supply ratio increases prices tend to rise. If the ratio decreases prices tend to fall. These tendencies depend on a finite supply of money in the consumer market.

But more interestingly, prices can rise even as demand falls, if supply falls off more rapidly. And prices can fall even as demand expands if supply expands more rapidly.

Politicians will often target a commodity in demand for tax revenues. Sin taxes will reduce both the supply of a commodity and the demand for it. But if a significant fall in demand does not follow a price increase (because of inelastic demand), sellers can pass their tax costs to buyers. Their competition is not with each other, their common cost is government.

The graduated income tax is one of the government's grandest scams. The tax maximizes government revenues and minimizes taxpayer resistance. It's a politicians dream. But supply and demand intervene. The apparent taxpayers are not often the real taxpayers.

Taxes are not passive players in the economic landscape. Graduated income taxes reduce the supply of people they target and raise the demand for them. The demand to supply ratio increases. Net pay sets the supply of professionals in the landscape. Gross pay sets their cost to consumers. Taxes on people in high economic demand are passed from seller to buyer in higher costs.

The graduated tax and trial lawyers are major contributors to the high costs of medical care. Excessive taxes, lawsuits, or other threats reduce the supply of medical doctors per capita and increase their costs to consumers.

Let us hope our clueless Congress does not attempt to expand medical care and pay for it with higher income tax brackets. The medical establishment will be decimated.

Witness what parliament has done to Canadian medicine. Recently (2005) the Supreme Court of Canada overturned the government monopoly on single payer health care systems in Quebec because waiting lists and long delays in health care delivery were resulting in thousands of deaths. First the unlimited demand for 'free care' swelled the costs to Ottawa. And then government cost controls targeting the providers of medicine reduced their supply. The demand to supply ratio soared.

Hooray for political boundaries. They illuminate gross government stupidity.

Chapter 14

The Nature of Money

Trade is an exchange of commodities between people. The first trades were probably exchanges of game or fruit among primitives. Trade allows a division of labor. Some could hunt and some could gather. Trade allows members of a society to concentrate on doing that which they do best. The primitive society experiences an immediate rise in their standard of living with the division of labor.

But an immediate obstacle to trade arises in a larger population. One may not want to trade his game which feeds many for fruit that feeds one. But they might trade by weight. Weight could be used to set values. But a non perishable or durable medium of exchange would be better.

A medium of exchange must be divisible. A small quantity must be available for the small trade, a larger quantity for the larger trade. And of course it must be rare. A rock will not do. One does not give up the fruit of ones labor for a common stone.

But for a precious stone one might. A precious stone has brilliance. It has color. It is a rock that one can peer into. And it is faceted, it is very mysterious. It will command a lot of game.

Gold is a rock also. Gold nuggets may be found pure in nature. While not faceted, gold is lustrous. It will not rot nor tarnish. It can be melted and shaped into coin. It seems indestructible.

But gold has a most mysterious property. It is extremely heavy. It is the heaviest natural substance known to men. Only platinum, iridium, and osmium are denser. But these elements are unknown. Gold weighs seven times as much as granite or marble.

A brick of butter will weigh one pound. A brick of gold will weigh twenty times as much.

Because of its density, gold cannot be faked. And its relative scarcity caused it to be coveted. Traders would accept gold in trade. Over time gold became a preferred medium of exchange. Gold became money.

Gold facilitated trade and trade grew with civilization. But even gold has its limits. A lot of gold is difficult to push around, let alone carry. Gold came to be stored in gold vaults and gold certificates were issued. The certificates are titles to a weight in gold. It is similar to having title to a home or a car.

The certificates were traded instead. A standard weight of gold or gold coin was payable to the certificate bearer on demand. The gold certificate was an entitlement to a weight of gold. There was a weight in gold somewhere in safe keeping that belonged to the bearer on demand.

Then governments entered the coin minting business. In America the feds initially issued twenty dollar gold certificates or one ounce gold coins in exchange for mined gold. One ounce of gold in coin was payable to the holder of a twenty dollar gold certificate. The feds also issued silver certificates and silver dollars. A one ounce silver dollar was payable to the holder of a one dollar silver certificate on demand. Then the Federal Reserve Note was introduced. Federal Reserve Notes were made equivalent to gold certificates and silver certificates. Fractional reserve banking was created.

In 1934 Roosevelt seized the gold holdings of Americans by severing the gold certificates title to a weight in gold. In 1971 Nixon seized the silver holdings of Americans in the same manner, completing the political debasement of the real money supply. Government has taken our gold and silver receipts and left us holding only Federal Reserve Notes.

By making the Federal Reserve Note legal tender one must accept the note as payment of debt. One may no longer demand gold or silver for reimbursement. Today your bank account is nothing but a score card. And your government is free to cheapen the value of the Federal Reserve Note and your bank account by printing money.

Is gold really necessary for money? The short answer is no. If we could trust the government not to counterfeit money on a grand scale, then Federal Reserve Notes are money substitutes. Unfortunately governments can never be trusted. Federal counterfeiting became necessary after corrupt politicians linked the money supply to employment with corrupt labor laws.

When governments go on a spending spree, as they are wont to do, they can spend gold or silver until they run out of gold or silver. Then they must stop spending. Or they can spend Federal Reserve notes until they run out of paper and ink. Governments never run out of paper and ink.

Before government monopolized the private sector's money, banks issued their own gold or silver certificates. The certificates given to customers were receipts for the metal which was taken and stored in the bank's vaults. Some bankers (lacking personal integrity) issued certificates in excess of their gold or silver holdings. This expands the money supply. The fraction of gold or silver held in reserve is less than the amount of gold or silver certificates in circulation. If depositors think their certificates could be bogus, they will initiate a run on the bank for the gold or silver that the notes entitle them to.

After the government monopolized the private sectors money, it issued the Federal Reserve Note. It is the same game by a different name. The practice is called fractional reserve banking.

With fractional reserve banking the amount of money in circulation can be expanded by issuing Federal Reserve Notes. Gold or silver holdings need only be a fraction of the money in circulation.

Today fractional reserve banking means only the fraction of deposits the bank must keep in reserve to meet its day to day operations. The fraction is no longer in gold or silver, it is in paper money.

The feds can expand the money supply in three ways. They can lower the discount rate, the interest rate they charge member banks for borrowing notes. They can lower the fraction of deposits member banks must keep in reserve. They can buy government securities on the open market (mostly Treasury bills). All methods create excess reserves and allow an expansion of the money supply.

The Congress will also engage in counterfeiting whenever Congressional spending exceeds tax revenues and borrowing. Deficit spending is their euphemism for authorizing the printing of reserve notes.

Private commerce can also expand the money supply. If one borrows money he can create a promissory note for it, like a share of stock. Such notes are entitlements to a share of the company and they may also promise interest. They are generally not used as money substitutes because their value is not fixed and they carry risk.

But Federal Reserve notes bear the warning, **legal tender for all debts public and private.** You must accept them for money. They do not promise interest and they carry enormous risk.

The Federal Reserve Note is a government issued IOU. One can merely hope that Federal Reserve Notes can be traded for something of value.

When gold or silver was money, the money supply could not be arbitrarily increased or decreased. It was a fixed commodity. But Federal Reserve notes are numbers on paper. So are checkable accounts. And the Federal Reserve multiplier readily changes the amount of money in circulation.

The value of money is set by supply and demand. The natural market will set buying power to allow all goods to be purchased. Let us imagine a society of six individuals and a gross national pie to buy. Each person shall initially possess one dollar. Each person has equal buying power. They will each be able to buy one sixth of the pie for one dollar each. It's the first law of Economics in a Nutshell.

Now we will double the money supply. Each individual will be given two dollars. Each individual may think he can now buy two pieces of the pie.

But he can't!

All six individuals still possess equal buying power. Doubling the money supply merely doubles prices. It will now take two dollars to buy what one dollar did before. The individual's share of the money supply remains his share of the market irregardless of inflation. Inflation will not by itself affect buying power.

In the real world prices rise over time as new money infuses into the market. The amount of money in circulation does not matter in the long run. But when it is increasing, the counterfeiter and the initial recipients gain. But what is gained by some will be lost to inflation by those who follow or those on fixed income. Counterfeiting is a zero sum game. Some win. Some lose.

The money supply can be drained from the market by the opposite measures that lead to expansion. The Federal Reserve can raise the prime rate of interest. Money costs more to borrow. Demand for loans will contract. Outstanding loans will be paid back. Federal Reserve notes are repossessed by the central banking system and destroyed. The money flow through corporate America will fall.

But will prices fall?

In an earlier time, a decreasing per capita money supply would cause wages and prices to fall in step (but not buying power). In these political times, labor laws will prevent the spreading of lower wages and inhibit the fall of prices. Employment will fall instead.

When the labor force shrinks, production shrinks and buying power shrinks. The result is **stagflation**, rising prices with unemployment.

John Maynard Keynes (revered British economist and darling of the political left) has said that a little bit of inflation is necessary to maintain employment. Keynes would have us believe that unemployment is a fault of free enterprise. It decidedly is not. It is a fault of politics. Unemployment is the unintended consequence of forcing the price of labor above the market ability to pay. Then the money supply must be increased to replace the surwages seized by organized labor. Did Keynes comprehend that Western governments were merely engaging in damage control?

Inflation, stagflation, wage gaps, recessions and depression are all caused by federal manipulation of the money supply in the presence of political wage supports.

Welcome to the fruits of Points Five and Eight of the Communist Manifesto. Your government adopted them.

Chapter 15

The Natural Distribution of Wealth

Let us look at the natural (not coerced) distribution of wealth. Let us assume that our society of six that we visited earlier is initially labor of equal skills and ambition. They produce an aggregate product that we shall again treat as a pie to be divided up. Since all laborers contribute equally, they will each earn one sixth of production. The pie will be sliced into six equal pieces. It is a 1, 1, 1, 1, 1, 1 distribution. This is an egalitarian distribution.

But the labor mix is ideal. It is not real. An egalitarian distribution is not possible. It is not even desirable. We are not clones. While we may envy our doctors share of national income, most of us are not prepared to share his responsibilities or his risks. Nor are we prepared to spend an additional decade of our time and money attaining his economic worth.

There are many measures of economic worth. In our society of six let us assume that one becomes an entrepreneur. By hiring two laborers and utilizing their labor in a more efficient manner, the entrepreneur doubles the production of the three of them from three pieces to six. The aggregate national product of the six increases to nine pieces. But how will the pie be distributed in the new economy?

We will assume the entrepreneur is able to keep two pieces out of six in profit. But the two laborers working for the entrepreneur have no more talent than the other three who work independently. They are interchangeable. Therefore the five laborers will divide the seven remaining pieces equally. The new distribution is **2.0**, 1.4, 1.4, 1.4, 1.4, and 1.4 (nine total). They experience a 40 percent rise in their standard of living.

The entrepreneur will experience a greater rise in his standard of living for his efforts. But the others will get their rise simply for living in the entrepreneurial society and sharing the entrepreneurial expansion. An intelligent society will put no limits on their entrepreneurs. They will go along for the ride.

Along come the socialists. The socialists see only the entrepreneur's gain. They cannot see societies gain as a result of entrepreneurial effort. Their greed blinds them. They will claim that the entrepreneur is hogging the wealth. It is the great socialist lie. They will attempt to pull themselves up by pulling the entrepreneur down.

The laborers form a labor union. They will demand a share of the entrepreneur's profit, but they won't earn it. They seize their share by threatening competitive labor with harm and the entrepreneur with losses. The coerced distribution is **2**, 2, 2, 1, 1, and 1 (again nine total).

The entrepreneur keeps his gains by entrepreneurial effort. His employees gain by coercion. But a huge wage gap has been opened between favored and non favored labor. Three laborers whose talents match the other two earn minimum wages. The socialists have divided labor between haves and have nots.

The union will hog the entrepreneurial abundance that supply and demand would naturally distribute to all labor in accordance with their efforts and ability (their market worth). The labor union had nothing to do with the increase in wealth, but it has everything to do with the unwarranted disparity in the distribution of wealth.

In economic life the best that one may hope for is that all wealth is _earned_. Earned wealth is never stolen. It arises from a personal response to economic demand.

Labor exists all over the world. Wealth does not. Entrepreneurs orchestrate an industrial process that creates wealth out of labor, material, and energy.

The entrepreneur by nature may keep only a fraction of his income in sales. But his gross sales are a measure of societies gain.

And his net income is both his incentive and his reward for contributing to society. The entrepreneur will produce as much as he can sell. Socialism offers no similar incentives or rewards. Socialism fails to grow.

Remember the First Law of Economics in a Nutshell. Prices must fall until all products are sold. And prices will fall if wages are not held above market by force of law. But the buying power of wages will rise with falling prices and rising employment.

Of course employment must rise in the private sector, not in government. The government sector produces no marketable goods. It produces only taxes or subsidies replete with threats and spirit draining red tape.

But entrepreneurs never gain by pulling others down. Entrepreneurs gain by pulling others up. Big time!

Chapter 16

The Entrepreneur and the Socialist

Labor has a value set by the market. The value is set by supply and demand. The entrepreneur does not determine market wages. But he must pay them. The entrepreneur profits by creating wealth for others. He shares his productivity with society. But that is not enough for some. The socialist will seek to share the entrepreneur's profits (but never his losses). He will pull himself up by pulling another down.

Let us compare the entrepreneur to the socialist worker. The entrepreneur takes the risks. The worker takes none. The entrepreneur is exposed to lawsuits for his and his employee's mistakes. The worker is shielded from lawsuits. The entrepreneur borrows money to invest in his enterprise. The worker borrows nothing. The entrepreneur may create a stock company to raise cash and invest his life savings into shares. The worker invests nothing in a share. The entrepreneur may invest 60 to 80 hours a week nursing his fledgling company. The worker nurses a beer at a ballgame. And at all times the entrepreneur must pay market wages irregardless of his financial condition.

Over time the successful entrepreneur builds a company and hires more labor.

Along come the Marxists. At some magic number of employees, the workers will be allowed to form a union and strike the company. So what do the socialists want for nothing?

The union will want to share in the profits, although they bought no stock and assumed no risk. They will claim they produced the product, but they only sold their labor. They will threaten to harm the company with a strike unless their demands are met. And in future strikes they must intimidate competitive labor from crossing picket lines for the wages coerced from the company.

An often used alibi is the little guy. The giant corporation steps on the <u>little guy</u>. It is incredible how people can think that the little guy (who uses the guns of government to sack his employer) is the victim.

Coercing excessive wages or benefits on a grand scale has egregious economic consequences. Wage gaps (minimum wages), recessions and depression (no wages), result from the mass taking of unearned surwages from the natural economy.

And as continuing wage coercion sends their former employer toward bankruptcy, politicians draft taxpayers to reward the perpetrators with government backed health and retirement insurance or a bankruptcy bailout.

This is your government at work.

Chapter 17

Balance of Trade

Now that we know the nature of money, recall that the price of American products is set by the money supply. If Americans purchase more foreign products than foreigners purchase from America then there is a net flow of money out of the country. This is a negative balance of trade.

Normally a negative balance of trade is not sustainable. Prices will fall as the money supply falls in house. That will make American products more competitive and the sale of foreign products to Americans will decrease. The sale of American products to foreigners will increase. The money flow will reverse. Trade is self balancing if government is not counterfeiting currency.

The same thing will occur if the nation is on a gold standard. Gold will neither accumulate nor disappear because of international trade, if the government honors the gold standard. Nations that counterfeit will see their gold stocks dwindle as creditors demand gold in exchange for counterfeit notes. Nations that don't won't.

So why give a damn about the balance of trade? No one should. But the political symbionts cannot tolerate deflation. Labor unions will fight the natural deflation of wages and prices when the balance of trade is negative and the money supply is falling. Their above market surwages (or their employment) would be the prime target of a natural decrease in the money supply.

Organized labor will fight the natural market avoidance of overpriced labor by targeting competitive trade. They participate in parades at world trade conferences. And some patsies of organized labor will engage in riots. Witness the Seattle meeting of the WTO on 30 November 1999.

And the feds will counter the offshore flow by expanding the money supply. That of course will continue the offshore flow. Witness the imbalance of trade.

A negative balance of trade cannot be continued forever. Part of the imbalance of trade (one hundred billion per annum) is in growing interest payments on federal debt notes held by foreign governments (mostly China and Japan).

America's trading partners are using their excess American dollars to buy debt instruments and American businesses. When we run out of assets to sell off, the dollar will collapse. Trade will collapse. And our industrial base will have completed its decimation at the hands of organized labor.

The Eurodollar should also collapse. Different governments in the European alliance will cheapen the Eurodollar unevenly causing wealth to flow from producing states towards the free loading states. The more productive states must drop out or be dragged down. That is why nations have always had their own currencies.

The balance of trade is never an economics problem per se. It is always caused by inflating the money supply. And in America it is the collusion of the Congress with organized labor that sustains the problem.

Chapter 18

Market Balance

There is always a natural downward pressure from buyers and a natural upward pressure from sellers on prices in a free economy. Competition will drive both wages and prices downward. <u>But shortages will drive them upward.</u>

So how far can wages and prices fall? To where all supplies are sold and all workers are hired. At clearance, prices have reached the margin of a market shortage. And at full employment, wages have reached the margin of a labor shortage. Neither wages nor prices can fall further.

The labor union will whine that employers would pay squat if not for union coercion. That is decidedly false. A balance between wage rates and employment always exists. But a balance at full employment is optimum. At full employment production and the buying power of wages are at their peak.

Prices balance buyers with sellers. If the money supply were to increase, wages and prices must both increase to maintain the balance.

There will never be enough wealth in the world to satisfy everyone's desires. The wealth must be rationed by some means. In free enterprise the money supply serves as ration coupons and earnings determine their distribution.

Free enterprise is a remarkable economic engine. Where there is a shortage of skills, public demand will raise the wages offered. And the supply of skills will increase because of the higher wages. A natural economy is directed from the bottom up. No bureaucracy can direct from the top down that which is easily and naturally directed by the sum of all voluntary exchanges between buyers and sellers at the grass roots level. Nor can a more fundamentally honest distribution of wages be made.

A fully employed society will create maximum affluence for its members and distribute the affluence **to each** in accordance with their ability. But the socialist creed demands **from each** in accordance with their ability. The fundamentally dishonest socialist will force apart the marriage of ability with incentive and decimate the production of affluence. An affluent middle class is a product of the free. Socialism has never produced an affluent society.

The capable will always contribute the most to a free society. They may accumulate wealth over time, but they deliver to the public a product of far greater value in the present. That is why the capable are in economic demand.

Unarmed free enterprise will create a natural and bountiful economic balance without economic knowledge. But political force and ignorance will destroy it.

Smugglers provide goods that government has banned or overtaxed. Liquor, fireworks, slot machines, and cigarettes for instance. American Indians are engaged in smuggling big time.

The black market provides goods and services priced at real market value. It provides items that are scarce because government forced their price below market. Like gas during Carter times!

Politically fixing prices above market will always result in surpluses. They won't sell (like overpriced labor). Politically fixing prices below market will always result in shortages. They won't be supplied. The intelligent society will allow the impersonal finesse of supply and demand to set wages for full employment and prices for market clearance.

Chapter 19

Velocity

Economic velocity is the number of times the money supply is exchanged per annum. It could be thought of as the average number of times a dollar passes from a buyer to a seller over the course of a year. To illustrate velocity we can assume a population of three farmers who specialize in different crops. They grow just enough for themselves and to sell to their neighbors. We may assume they plant a spring and a fall crop. There will be two harvests per year.

Let us assume that each farmer has two dollars to spend. The money supply in this example is six dollars. At spring harvest time each farmer will buy a dollars worth of food from each of the other two. The three will spend six dollars total. And each farmer will earn two dollars from sales of his own crop to the other two. At fall harvest time they will repeat the exchange. The three have now spent twelve dollars in their farm year. The money supply remains at six dollars, so its velocity is two exchanges per annum.

One may note that if the initial money supply was tripled, each sale would have cost three dollars instead of one. Prices are set by the money supply. The velocity however will not change. Velocity is set by farm production. It will remain at two exchanges of the money supply per year irregardless of the money supply.

The lesson here is that prices and velocity are independent variables. Prices are proportional to the money supply. Velocity is proportional to productivity and employment. A change in one will have no direct effect on the other.

These farmers could drop back to one crop per year or rev up to three seasonal crops per year greatly affecting velocity but without affecting prices. The reader should keep this in mind when he reads the chapter on the federally alleged overheated economy.

Chapter 20

The Equation of Inflation

Velocity is the number of times the money supply is exchanged per year. It is calculated by dividing the total amount of money paid by all consumers for retail products per annum (GNP) by the money supply. It is measured in exchanges per year.

Since the federal bashing of the economy in the year 2000 economic velocity has fallen by about 25 percent but inflation continues. Can we still conclude that inflation is independent of velocity? Absolutely!

In our farming community we determined that inflation does not arise out of an increase in velocity. They are independent variables. But velocity does reflect man hours of employment and community output.

Our present interest is in revealing how velocity affects employment and how the money supply affects inflation on a national scale. We shall look at the role of velocity in the equation of inflation to clarify its independence.

The author will use the term Aggregate Price Paid for the cost of all retail purchases made over a year and Aggregate Product Sold for the amount purchased. Does the Aggregate Product Sold truly represent what Americans purchase with American money per annum? How should exports and imports be treated?

Trade replaces exports with imports. It substitutes foreign products for American products. It's a trade. And if we import more products than we export, then we export money. So the aggregate product sold will still represent the supply of goods in the American market to be purchased with the money remaining in house. And the ratio of the amount paid in dollars to the quantity purchased still provides a real price index and a measurement of inflation.

Prices are measured in dollars per purchase on the small scale, like the Bureau of Labor Statistics infamous market basket invented for indexing inflation. But the big basket is the sum of all the little market baskets.

The average price level is equal to the aggregate price paid for consumer products per annum (demand) divided by the aggregate product sold (supply). The quotient in dollars per annual purchase provides a domestic measure of inflation. The algebraic relation is shown below.

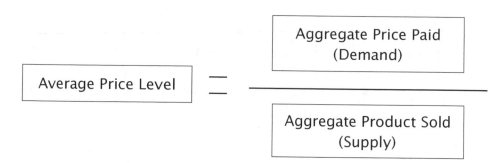

Inflation cheapens the dollar. More dollars are required to purchase a fixed amount of goods and services. The average price level will rise year after year. But what is the source of inflation?

Recall that velocity is the number of times the money supply is spent per annum. Both man hours worked and man hours paid rise and fall together. But man hours worked affects market supply and man hours paid affects market demand. Barring dramatic shifts of labor from private productivity to political larceny, supply and demand will also rise and fall together and a change in velocity by itself cannot affect the demand to supply ratio.

Thus the average price level generally remains independent of velocity, directly proportional to the money supply, and inversely proportional to market abundance.

Again we conclude that prices do not inflate with velocity. Prices inflate with the money supply.

However, the feds recently (2000) linked market velocity to inflation. They propagated the myth of an <u>overheated economy</u>. And they slammed the money supply, slowed the economy, and brought down the stock market. The reverberations continue still. That great alibi and the feds self serving motive for bringing down the stock market will be revealed later.

Chapter 21

The Equation of Employment

The average hourly wage in America is equal to the aggregate sum of all wages paid over a given interval divided by the sum of all man hours worked during the interval. By expressing employment in terms of man hours, we arrive at the equation of employment below.

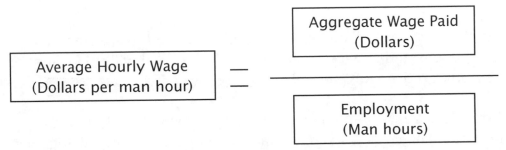

If the aggregate wage paid isummed over a year, the divisor is the sum of all hours worked per annum. But one man year (2000 man hours) is also a job. It is clear that our divisor in man hours is also a measure of employment.

One may note the relation of the quotient to the divisor. The average hourly wage is inversely proportional to employment in man hours. They are locked in this relationship by a finite money supply and consequently a finite aggregate wage. An inverse relationship between variables means that if one of the variables (average hourly wage) is raised by law, the other variable (employment in man hours) must decrease.

If the feds increase the money supply, the aggregate wage paid can climb. Wage rates and employment are then both free to rise. If wage rates are frozen, employment can climb a lot. Wage rates and man hours of employment remain inversely related. But if the new money goes into wage rates instead of rising employment, prices will inflate (stagflation).

The feds cannot steer new money away from surwage labor toward new and more productive jobs. The political power of organized labor to seize surwages will limit job creation and inflate prices.

Without government inflation everyone would know the Second Law of Economics in a Nutshell. And everyone would know that the sum of all wages is limited by the money supply. And employment is normally unlimited.

There are no wages being held back in deep pockets anywhere. There never has been. Wages are always fully deployed. The impression that more wages are earned in good times than in bad is true. But it arises out of an increase in velocity.

The coerced surwages of organized labor arise out of the potential wages or jobs of others. Wage inflation may conceal the fall of real wages for the many, but it cannot conceal unemployment. The redistribution of wages from low paid labor to high paid labor, by organized labor, is the least recognized and most despicable covert relationship in the political landscape.

The feds can periodically expand the money supply to fund the jobs lost to wage coercion. But the wage gaps opened by the coercion will also expand. And the middle class will shrink. Only the Congress could close the unearned wage gaps. But the Congress will do no such thing. The Congressional puppets dance on the strings of organized labor.

Minimum wage laws represent damage control. They were first promoted by American Communists in the nineteen twenties. In the twenties, the wage gaps seeded by politicians and organized labor began to flower. Private enterprise took the blame. In 1938 the Fair Labor Standards Act introduced the minimum wage. It represented an absurdity whose need was created by the earlier economic folly of the United States Congress.

What is economically desirable is to prohibit wage coercion and let minimum wages rise as above market wages decline. A natural minimum wage would be much higher and fairer in buying power than are the minimum wages of today.

The socialist will dance forever around the inverse relation between wage demands and employment. But his greed will not let him recognize it. He prefers to believe that he is mining deep pockets.

But wages do not come from deep pockets. Wages come from corporate sales. Their source is consumer pockets.

Chapter 22

The Monopoly

Many people have played the Parker Brothers board game of Monopoly. But do they know that the game does not resemble free enterprise in any manner? The Monopoly player cannot avoid losses if a roll of the dice puts him in harms way. The game shows us how free choice must be restricted to allow a monopoly to arise.

Monopolies abound in the landscape. All of them have government protection. Some of the largest monopolies include,

- Transportation unions and their monopoly on transportation.
- The legal monopoly and their unlimited reach for damages.
- Education associations and their monopoly on education.
- Police and firemen unions and their protection monopolies.
- American Indians and their monopoly on land, game, and fisheries.
- Professional sports and their monopoly on franchises

In all cases it is competition that must be curbed by law to create the monopoly. A monopoly cannot exist in free enterprise. Monopolies are backed by gun.

Picket lines are of utmost importance for protecting union labor from competitive labor. Other methods of life support used to sustain the monopoly include tariffs, import quotas, tax exemptions, subsidies, licensing, certification, and permits. Smuggling, black marketing, scalping, scabbing, and operating or practicing without a license, are crimes invented by government to curb competition in the market. Not surprisingly, it is the strongest competition that is often accused by the uncompetitive of engaging in monopoly.

The Spanish economist, Faustino Ballvé, declared it impossible to find a monopoly that does not enjoy state protection.[7] His treatise on economics

[7] Faustino Ballvé, "Essentials of Economics," The Foundation for Economic Education, Inc., Irvington on Hudson, New York, 1994, pg. 54.

has been published in three languages because of its acclaim in Western Europe.

If monopolies cannot exist without government protection, why does the Justice Department have an anti trust division? Why was Microsoft in the government's gun sights? What is the purpose of the anti trust act?

Irregardless of published intention, it is used to protect the uncompetitive from free market competition and to attract funds for the enhancement of Congressional careers.

Once upon a time in America, **coal** was the major currency of energy. Coal was from West Virginia. But there was a young rival in the landscape. It was **oil**. Standard Oil was from New Jersey. Coal needed protection.

Coal found John Sherman. John sponsored the Sherman Antitrust Act. It was enacted in 1890. It would shortly target Standard Oil of New Jersey for breakup as an alleged monopoly. Sherman represented West Virginia in the United States Senate. One could say that Sherman represented his state well by assaulting the competition. But his consumer bashing activity was all politics. It was not economics.

Standard Oil was accused of predatory price cutting. This is an alleged practice of lowering prices below that of rivals until they fold and then raising prices in a market bereft of competition. But that never happens. When prices rise, other sellers enter the market. Predatory price cutting is known as an alibi.

The price of kerosene had fallen by two thirds over three decades in the late nineteenth century. Rockefeller had earned most of the market when he was slammed by the Sherman Act.[8]

Thus we have an alleged crime, monopoly. We have an alleged perpetrator, oil. And we have an alleged victim, coal. Oil committed monopoly.

Actually, oil committed competition.

---

[8] Lawrence W. Reed, "Remembering a Classic That Demolished a Myth," Human Events, 02 October 98, pg. 15.

And more recently Microsoft committed competition. For their effort Microsoft has come under assault both at home and abroad. But Microsoft is unarmed. Monopolies require the force of law or outlaw. Who is holding the gun?

A number of software companies including major competitors of Microsoft are located in Utah. They called on their senator, Orrin Hatch, for help. Orrin chaired the Senate Judiciary Committee at the time. Orrin emerged as one of Microsoft's most outspoken critics.

And Microsoft is located in Washington State. Where were our senators while Microsoft was under political assault? Perhaps they were out fund raising.

And the business of the Justice Department appears to be the protection of the uncompetitive rather than the promotion of competition. The uncompetitive will shop for political protection. The competitive don't need political protection.

The Supreme Court has exempted sports from the Sherman Act. The court has ruled that a sport is not a business. But as soon as one erects a fence around the ball park and charges admission fees, the sport enters the entertainment business.

By limiting major league franchises, the sports monopoly excludes any nearby competition in the market and raises the price of admission. Ball player salaries reveal monopoly influence. Umpire salaries will also. Major league ballparks have become the gladiatorial arenas of the wealthy. The rest of us watch the games and bear the commercials on the boob tube.

Fans may voluntarily support millionaires, but the taxpayers should not have to. But the taxpayer is forced to fund the construction of stadiums with their viewing suites for the benefit of team owners and their political patrons.

Owners and players pocket admission charges, owners avoid property taxes, taxpayers pay the rent, and politicians typically acquire box seats as a freebie.

Monopolies always enjoy government protection. No monopoly is possible in free enterprise. Competition must always be inhibited by law or outlaw to form a monopoly.

Chapter 23

The Wealthy

Wealth is not money. Wealth is the output of the corporate world. It has an intrinsic value that is independent of inflation. Most wealth is not permanent. It depreciates with age. Homes, home furnishings, and automobiles are examples of wealth that fades with time. Real estate and gold are examples of durable wealth. They do not depreciate with time.

Most of the wealth, in any society that possesses it, is held by the aged. The working young may have their homes and cars. But they also have their mortgages and car payments. They are renters. The salient character of the wealthy is that most spent a working life earning and accumulating their wealth and their retirement.

There are exceptions. There are sports figures in the sports monopolies and there are celebrities. These people gain wealth early in life. They often gain wealth before wisdom. Their wealth provides them a pulpit from which they often espouse economic nonsense.

Consumer advocate Ralph Nader has criticized Microsoft Chairman Bill Gates and other billionaires in the world for hogging the wealth of the nation and the globe.[9] This is the socialist mentality, the mentality of scarcity. Their gain must have been at the expense of another. But honest income is never taken from another, it is earned.

Gates owns a significant portion of Microsoft, a company he and others created. His share of Microsoft stock is his wealth. But the wealth created by Microsoft is shared by the world. Creating consumer wealth is the only way an honest individual in a free society can gain wealth.

An increase in honestly earned income flowing from buyer to seller is always accompanied by an increase in products flowing in the opposite direction from seller to buyer. Economically the counter flow represents an increase

---

[9] "Nader suggests Gates, others spread wealth," Associated Press, Cited in The Sun, 28 July 98.

in velocity and in productivity. The money remains in circulation. Nothing is lost. A lot is gained. This is a good thing.

Nader mixes privately earned wealth with seized wealth when he bundles all the wealthy into one bag. Many politicians around the globe are billionaires. They seize money under color of law and they return little if anything to the market. This is decidedly bad.

Socialists gain wealth by pulling down others. Their intellect or their indolence will not include effort as a means of gain. They seek to use legality and malice. The legality removes the retribution. The malice arises out of ignorant hate. All socialists are engaged in hate crime.

The wealthy may buy the first automobiles, the first refrigerators, the first airline tickets, and the first personal computers. But their purchases create an economic demand for progress.

The wealthy pay the developmental cost of new products. They buy the latest and greatest. Later buyers must only sustain the cost of production. They pay only a fraction of first article cost.

There is more. A significant portion of personal wealth funds charity or is reinvested in private enterprise where it funds material, facilities, or labor. The poor society has no such capital resource.

And the wealthy add value to the dollar, whereas government always cheapens the tax dollar by removing it from the production of wealth.

The American Gross National Product per capita is several hundred times that of some third world countries. The peasants in third world countries work harder and longer than do the unskilled in America, yet they remain poor. Obviously wealth does not arrive out of labor. It is money invested in corporate America that provides the machinery of wealth.

Interestingly the per capita output of America is less than that of Switzerland or Japan. And these countries possess no fossil fuel resources. The reason we are no longer first in the world is squatting on the Potomac.

In a free enterprise society the older generation leads the young. The young are simply a generation behind in sharing the affluence. Those who wait for wealth to rain down on them call it trickle down. They will wait forever. And that is truly their problem.

But those who earn could accumulate more wealth and do it sooner than the preceding generation has. And they will if the growth of government and the seizure of taxes do not impoverish their efforts.

Chapter 24

The Nature of Competition

In free enterprise the competition for sales will drive prices downward until all products are sold. Prices can fall no further. It's the first law of Economics in a Nutshell. Yet how many people believe that corporations (such as oil companies) are free to charge as they please?

Anyone who has tried to sell an old house or old car knows that if he sets the price too high he will find no buyers. The price is determined by the buyer. And there is no land fill anywhere where new products are being buried for lack of buyers.

The last paragraph says it all. Buyers force prices down to a level where profits to sellers are minimized. But they cannot push prices down further. The number of sellers would fall. The ratio of buyers to sellers (demand to supply) would rise and halt the fall in prices. It's a natural balance.

The seller of a good has much more of his product than he needs or wants. The Sunday paper is filled with advertisements for sales. Sellers are easy targets for buyers. It's a buyers market.

A sellers market only occurs when there are shortages. Shortages can be caused by earthquake, hurricane, flood, or gold rush. But they often occur as the unintended consequence of price controls. Normally a shortage will raise prices and higher prices will attract more sellers. That will <u>snuff out the shortage</u>. The crisis quickly passes. In free enterprise prices have nothing to do with greed; they have everything to do with balance. That is the unique role of prices.

But moronic government will heroically demand lower prices, threaten potential suppliers with scalping prohibitions and fines, and <u>snuff out the recovery</u>.

The money supply is exchanged perhaps two times per year. Economists call it velocity. In the exchange money flows from buyer to seller and a product flows from seller to buyer in the opposite direction. Thus velocity is tied intrinsically to production and is independent of the money supply.

But the sum of all prices is related to the money supply.

Because the money supply is finite, sales are always inversely proportional to prices. If the producer raises his real price (in excess of inflation) his sales will fall. If sales fall the producer must cut back on production, lay off employees, and sell off unused assets. No producer wants to downsize his business. He will attempt to maintain his share of the market by cutting his costs and his prices.

Heroic measures need not be taken to separate Coke and Pepsi, or to separate Texaco and Exxon. The Seattle Seahawks can compete with the Grand Canyon. People can choose to buy season tickets or take a vacation. Competition is not limited to product lines. Competition is across the board. In unadulterated free enterprise all sellers compete for buyers in the market.

Enter the adulterer. An ignorant and vicious liar, the United States government, will force itself upon the natural economy.

The United States government will legislate, regulate, litigate, and masturbate the natural economy. It will tax human effort and reward indolence. It will fiddle with wage and price supports. It will diddle with the money supply. And when inflation, stagflation, wage gaps, recessions, and depression arise as unintended consequences, the government will deploy its grand alibi.

Private enterprise did it!

A favorite political invention is the natural monopoly. Energy companies, water companies, and others are given all consumers residing within a specific region. But competition would arise at the borders if they were not fixed by law.

Competition arises naturally in free enterprise. But competition is not required to limit the average price level. That is the sole role of the money supply.

Competition is required to promote the efficient use of labor and natural resources and to inhibit waste and wasted effort. That increases human productivity. And human productivity enhanced by technology and energy creates the affluent and charitable society.

But the money supply cannot limit prices if the money supply itself is expanding. Our money supply is no longer a fixed quantity of gold or silver. It is paper. The feds are counterfeiting money and inflating prices across the board under the political euphemism of monetary policy.

Chapter 25

The Wages of Labor

In free enterprise the competition for jobs will drive wages downward until all labor is hired. Wages can fall no further. It's the second law of Economics in a Nutshell. Wages like prices will find a natural economic balance without political interference.

Corporate America earns its income in sales. Inside the corporation income is divided into tax and labor costs. To be sure there are other costs such as energy and material. But energy and matter are raw materials provided by nature. Their market value arises out of labor and tax costs that are forwarded to the point of sale with the finished product.

Because prices are a finite quantity constrained by the money supply, wages are a finite quantity constrained by corporate sales and corporate costs.

In free enterprise wages are normally distributed in proportion to the economic value of the labor purchased. There can be no finer or more productive way of distributing income and creating abundance.

But significant numbers of people will seize the potential wages of others if they can do so without the threat of retribution. They only require a means. Labor unions will fund the reelection campaigns of politicians. And politicians will permit strikes to intimidate employers and picket lines to intimidate competitive labor. It is quid pro quo. But it is also a negative sum game.

Wage rates and employment are always inversely related. The sum of all incomes (earned or seized under color of law) cannot exceed the money supply and its velocity. The coercion of surwages for some results in wage gaps and unemployment for others. The government will counter the unemployment that surwages create by periodically inflating the money supply. Americans consequently suffer surges of inflation. And the wage gaps continue to widen.

Part iv.
Labor Unions

We have briefly examined the economic fallacy of political wage supports. But does the coercion of surwages amount to extortion? It does in earlier times and in other places. But since 1914 the coercion of surwages is legal in America.

Few could have foreseen the immense economic disaster, which arming a private collective with the political power to seize surwages, would bring upon a free people. The Great Depression was just a foretaste of things to come. And the Congress is institutionally incapable of harnessing the evil they have released into the economic landscape.

Chapter 26

Affluence and the Surwages of Labor

Consider the economic effects of forceful redistribution. When a dollar is diverted from someone who would earn it and given to another who would not earn it, a dollars worth of effort is lost. The government takes hundreds of billions of tax dollars from economic production per annum and redistributes them as unearned entitlements. Unearned entitlements represent huge losses in potential human wealth.

In a similar manner organized labor removes huge amounts of consumer dollars from production and redistributes them as unearned surwages.

How is it done? Labor unions are allowed to strike and to set up picket lines. Competitive labor will be intimidated by picket line toughs. The employer will be threatened with huge economic losses in downtime. Company property may suffer inexplicable sabotage. The company will yield and the union will gain more in wages than their labor is valued on the market.

This short term gain for the union symbionts is also a long term loss for the company. The company's future is decimation, bankruptcy, or taxpayer bailout.

While the market value of wages is earned, the surwage (the amount above market value) is seized by politically allowed threat and intimidation. It is not pay for effort. Earned wages produce affluence. Surwages do not. Consumers must pay more than a free market price for their purchases from the surwage plagued corporation.

And when the consumer is required to pay more for union products, he is left with less money to purchase the products and fund the efforts of others. Money that should have created affluence will not. In this manner the surwage is diverted from production. Unearned surwages, like unearned entitlements, represent huge losses in potential human wealth.

Surwages and entitlements do just the opposite of what the socialists claim them to do, they increase poverty.

To maintain employment in the presence of continuing surwage demands that exceed the wage supply (demands not possible without threat and intimidation), a periodic expansion of the money supply is required. Surwages must come from somewhere. A natural economy cannot sequester wages. The wages must be taken from low paid labor or from the printing press. When unemployment rises, the Federal Reserve must increase the money supply to counter the hogging of wages by organized labor. Wage gaps continue to widen. And inflation becomes the norm.

Inflation is a legacy of organized labor and their political authority to strike. So are wage gaps. Private enterprise has nothing to do with the presence of wage gaps or inflation. It's the Congress. And the worst is yet to come.

Chapter 27

The Great Lie of Marxism

It should be self evident that a fair wage is one which neither employer nor employee was forced to accept. It is a wage set by mutual agreement between buyer and seller.

So why does any labor union call their wages unfair when their income far exceeds that of other workers for the same effort? Why do the unions seek to conceal rather than reveal their alleged unfair wage? What is the real purpose of the picket line?

Unfair is an alibi. Organized labor must conceal their real wage. The company must be seen as a greedy master and the employee as a wage slave. Competitive labor must be denigrated as scabs and intimidated from job seeking. That is the purpose of the picket line.

Scabs are portrayed as a lower form of life. They must be denied the high paid jobs coerced from the company. The politicians must receive their campaign funds from unions. The unions must receive political authority to coerce wages above market. And government controlled schools will preach the great economic falsehood for allowing such vicious behavior.

Politicians have alleged that there is a natural disparity in bargaining power between the individual and the large corporation. The corporation is seen as a collective while the worker is seen as an individual. Allowing workers to organize into a collective and engage in collective bargaining is proposed as a means to equalize economic power between employers and employees. [10]

But there is no natural disparity in economic power. The political ideology is that of Marx. Supply and demand sets wages. Employers cannot. Employers must pay market wages to hire workers and employees must accept market wages to find jobs. But politically favored labor can coerce surwages if they are empowered to threaten the corporation with harm.

Labor relation laws were enacted by the Congress to secure campaign contributions and Congressional careers. There is no economic justification for them. Election funding is the motive of the Congress. Greed is the motive of labor unions.

There is no natural disparity in economic power between the buyers and sellers of labor. Power is always political. Labor unions have created chronic unemployment by pricing union labor above the market supply of wages. This cannot happen in free enterprise. It requires political coercion.

The aggregate wage in the economic landscape is always a finite quantity related to the money supply and velocity. Jobs did not have to be. The great lie about the lack of bargaining power of an individual, laid the foundation for wage gaps, unemployment, recessions, and depression.

The great masses of the people...will more easily fall victim to a great lie than to a small one.
Adolph Hitler

Unemployment puts unskilled labor in a buyers market. But a shortage of talent will keep professional labor in a sellers market. The alleged natural disparity in economic power between employer and employee does not arise in a sellers market. That fact by itself reveals that an alleged economic disparity between the collective and the individual in bargaining power is bogus.

---

[10] Howell, Allison, and Henley, "The Legal Environment of Business," Second Edition, The Dryden Press, New York, 1987, p.307.

Full employment would put all labor in a sellers market. But a real political disparity has been enacted by government between union labor and non union labor. Consequently non union labor will fall as union labor rises. The wage gaps continue to widen. The middle class shrinks.

We shall visit that government euphemism that politicians have labeled collective bargaining next.

Chapter 28

Collective Bargaining

Collective Bargaining is a government created euphemism for coercive bargaining. It conceals labor union coercion and conduct behind closed doors. But there is no free bargaining. There is only demand, threat, and capitulation.

In 1995, the International Association of Machinists and Aerospace Workers at Boeing went out on strike. Boeing was making huge profits. The labor union wanted a share. That investors provided Boeing with the capital to purchase facilities, material, and labor, meant nothing to the labor union. They were prepared to coerce higher wages merely on the basis that the company was experiencing success. Labor took the credit.

The labor union possesses an arrogance arising from its political power. They will claim they built the aircraft. But of course they did no such thing. The company built the aircraft using labor, facilities, capital, and other resources that the company contracted, assembled, scheduled, and directed over a period of years. That is the role of corporate management.

One does not throw labor and material into a bag, shake it, and pour out a state of the art product. Unskilled labor is the least significant ingredient.

But political power will allow labor to close down the plant and establish picket lines. The purpose of the picket line is to interdict and intimidate competitive labor. But few manning the picket line would assault competitive labor over a market wage. Nor would competitive labor represent a serious threat to job holders in a free market. Picket line violence is the ugly fruit of coercing wages above market value, creating wage gaps between those possessing equal skills, and denying jobs to the unemployed at the wages offered.

Our union controlled schools teach us that labor laws were enacted to minimize labor strife. Ahem. Surwages maximize labor strife. Surwages attract the competition. The union guy walking the picket line knows his coerced income greatly exceeds his real market value and if he loses his job he won't command the same pay somewhere else. He will intimidate the competition and he will denigrate them as scabs.

Damage control legislation must follow the Clayton Act to contain the malice arising at the bargaining table and on the picket line. The union is not a stockholder nor is it a competent corporate manager. Yet they control the corporation's destiny. That destiny is decimation, bankruptcy, or bailout.

The corporation must entice thousands of workers to cross picket lines before it can resume operations. It's an impossible task. The picket line is a mob. Intimidation is their purpose. The exclusion of competitive labor will assure that coercion prevails at the bargaining table.

The Clayton Act was enacted in 1914. In section 6 of the act, the Congress exempted labor unions from anti trust law. Under the exemption, labor unions can use political weapons such as strikes and pickets without violating the Sherman Act or other anti trust legislation.[11]

Labor may not legally organize a small workforce. The corner grocery is exempt. Pickets are not allowed to threaten family owned businesses. The resemblance to an old fashioned protection racket would be remarkable. Politicians are eager to avoid the comparison. Collective bargaining will be limited by law to the larger workforce (with greater amounts of campaign cash).

More damage control is necessary when the corporation loses its market share. The union hides the coercion of surwages and the corporation's resultant fall in the market by accusing the competition of misconduct. The competition is dumping goods on the market. This is called an alibi.

---

[11] Howell, Allison, and Henley, "The Legal Environment of Business," Second Edition, Dryden Press, New York, 1987, p.545.

Labor negotiations also reveal the ugly face of coercion. Unlike any other bargaining between buyers and sellers in the free market, collective bargaining is unfriendly and vicious. A childhood friend who participated on a union bargaining team described the negotiations. Participants screamed obscenities at each other. The alleged bargaining was savage.

Another friend, who was in civil service management, described the hostile attitude towards his proposals for getting the job done in fewer hours. His budget was not of concern to the labor representatives. Slowdowns and overtime were the modus operandi of their union. The taxpayers could afford it. They feared no prosecution by law or firing by management. They were backed by political authority.

Collective bargaining is always conducted in private. Airing of the proceedings is not allowed. Federal mediators are present to contain the anger and confine it behind closed doors. The corporation has been targeted for harm.

Labor brings no promise of productivity to match wage demands to the bargaining table. Labor brings nothing to trade. The labor union brings only the threat of immediate harm to their employer if their demands are not met. Unfortunately they bring the threat of long term harm if their demands are met.

Demands! The word itself reveals the nature of collective bargaining.

The union is arrogant and the meeting not on fair terms. The company is negotiating its surrender. The company may not hire other labor at market value.

One should not expect collective bargaining to be cordial. One labor act after another was enacted in the twenties and thirties to control and conceal the malice arising out of collective bargaining and to prohibit business retribution. It continues still. Damage control is a continuous Congressional pastime. But the damage inflicted on the nation by organized labor will eventually overwhelm the damage control counter measures enacted by Congress.

It could be informative to watch the French. The French may be the first to experience the terminal agony of arming unelected Marxist labor unions with the political power to seize unearned surwages.

O what tangled webs we weave when first we practice to deceive.

Chapter 29

More Damage Control

We have seen how labor union pursuit of unearned surwages cheapens the dollar and widens wage gaps. We have seen the need for damage control legislation to conceal the savage nature of collective bargaining. Let us briefly visit some of the enormous damage control projects our government is mired in, by courtesy of the Clayton Act.

The Railway labor Act was passed in 1926 and is the basic statute governing labor relations in the rail industry. It was a blue print for the National Labor Relations Act (1935). By 1970 the railroad unions had seized so much in surwages, benefits, health care, pensions, and featherbedding that American railroads were failing. Amtrak was created to bail out the passenger industry. For forty years the Amtrak symbionts have promised to earn a profit and for forty years they have failed. Hello! Organized labor has taxpayers by the gonads. The railroad will never see a profit.

In 1974 the Pension Benefit Guarantee Corporation was created by the Congress to basically insure the lavish pensions of labor unions. Again federal taxpayers have been selected to bailout overpriced labor.

Labor costs forced Chrysler to the brink of bankruptcy in 1984. An import quota placed on Japanese imports by Reagan and a taxpayer bailout orchestrated by the Congress saved Chrysler. The demands of the United Auto Workers (UAW) had nearly bankrupted the auto giant. The increase in the price of domestic and imported cars as a result of quotas was over four billion dollars. This cost to American car buyers amounted to over 150,000 dollars per auto worker per year while the quotas were in effect.[12]

The Voluntary Employees Beneficiary Association (VEBA) was organized in 2007. General Motors and the United Auto Workers created this union operated organization to assume some 50 billion dollars of health care liabilities for present and former company employees. GM funded the new entity with 30 some billion dollars.

Obviously VEBA will be unable to fund their obligation, but then they do not expect to. The political left will emphasize a desperate need for national health insurance in federal election campaigns. Their greed will be cloaked in the needs of the self inflicted, in the needs of the unemployed, and in the needs of millions of illegal aliens who have crashed our borders. And the UAW expects to sneak in below the radar.

Thirty one American steel producers have filed for bankruptcy in the last four years (2002). The labor unions and the industry seek tariff protection. They say that foreign governments unfairly subsidize the competition.[13]

American made steel is not competitive because steel buyers must pay surwage costs at the point of sale. Americans should pay neither subsidy nor surwage. And if corrupt foreign governments want to subsidize our steel purchases from them, let that be their problem.

We are the world's largest trader and we are bordered by two oceans and a sea. Yet less than four percent of American shipping is conveyed on American vessels. The maritime industry was decimated by the unbridled demands of maritime unions. Its corpse is protected by maritime laws.

Big labor downsized the steel industry, the ship building industry, the maritime industry, and others. They are still downsizing the American owned auto and aircraft industries. These industries were the worlds largest at one time, but the surwages of organized labor are destroying them.

In November of 2008, immediately following the election of their 800 million dollar candidate for president of the United States, the political left

---

[12] David N. Hyman, "Economics", sec. ed., (Irwin), p. 169.

[13] Mike Allen and Steven Pearlstein, "Tariffs placed on imported steel by U.S.," The Washington Post, cited in The Sun, 06 March 02, pg. B1.

began demanding their payback. The United Auto Worker millionaires (in labor and management) had bankrupted General Motors. They required another bailout from taxpayers. The Democrats in the Congress emoted profusely about mismanagement before the cameras but they delivered on the investment big labor had made in them. They dance on the strings of organized labor.

Congressional bailouts will cause unemployment to soar as billions of dollars in taxes and surwages are removed from economic productivity. Price inflation arising from the drop in productivity will further lower economic velocity. And monetary inflation arising from printing bailout money will further depress market demand and result in raging stagflation. We have reached the limits of damage control. The seizure of surwages by organized labor must cease.

The first depression will be discussed in a later chapter.

A labor surplus is always caused by forcing labor costs above market value. And for nearly a century government has put people back to work by replacing the surwages seized by organized labor with minimum wages and wage gaps.

Stimulus spending is not the answer. The middle class has been plundered. A permanent stimulus will be required. That can only happen with a reduction in the size and appetite of government at all levels.

And the government cannot inflate unemployment away because an inflating stock market will threaten the national debt (as it did in 2000). The bastards are in a bind. The Congressional debt will be defaulted.

Union bosses are not unaware of the destruction of organized labor. They have moved to funding overpriced labor, their featherbedding, their unearned and outrageous pensions, and their health care benefits with taxpayer bailouts (Obama care) in perpetuity. They have found their deep pockets. Unlike consumers, the taxpayers cannot avoid the costs of overpriced government.

And how convenient can collective bargaining get between politicians and tax supported labor unions? They grease each others palms. Taxpayers are not present at the bargaining table.

Chapter 30

Coercion Begets Violence

Are you still unconvinced about the egregious nature of collective bargaining and legalized coercion, dear reader? Consider these United States Supreme Court decisions.

> ...**Linn recognized that Federal law gives a union license to use intemperate, abusive, or insulting language without fear of restraint or penalty if it believes such rhetoric to be an effective means to make its point.** [14]

Now you understand why 'collective bargaining' must be conducted behind closed doors. There is no slander in the inner sanctum. The intemperate, abusive, or insulting language employed by union officials and the intimidation of company representatives in attendance is concealed from public scrutiny.

> **The Hobbs Act, which makes it a federal crime to obstruct interstate commerce by robbery or extortion, does not reach the use of violence...to achieve legitimate union objectives...** [15]
>
> **To punish persons for such acts of violence was not the purpose of the Hobbs Act.** [16]

The use of violence to achieve 'legitimate' union objectives is allowed by the court. It's a license to kill. And if the feds are enjoined from prosecuting labor violence, the states are effectively hobbled also.

Coercion is not effective without intimidation. Intimidation is necessary. But coercion descends into violence when intimidation fails. And beating up scabs is an effective means of promoting intimidation.

---

[14] Cited from Letter Carriers v. Austin, 418 US 264.

[15] Cited from US v Enmons, 410 US 396.

[16] Ibid.

Labor unions formally do not sanction violence as a means to meet union objectives. They legally employ coercion. But coercion can erupt into violence where the coercion is seen as illegitimate or unjustified. That is the economic argument presented in this writing.

Human Events (1997) reported that nearly 9000 acts of violence by union toughs had occurred since 1975. The 9000 incidents constitute a small sample of police reports. Far more incidents are unreported in the news.[17]

In local television news (September 2000), a man had his trailer home vandalized by thugs. The thugs scribbled **scab** in blood red on his walls. Their victim had accepted a job at a Seattle steel mill that was suffering a strike.

There will be no real effort to bring the thugs to justice. The political establishment is not eager to hassle a campaign finance resource. Until economics overrides politics, labor union coercion will sporadically result in violence. And wage gaps and unemployment will feed the flames.

Violence and a maldistribution of income are burdens our society must bear to sustain the political careers of politicians.

Chapter 31

Child Labor

The Christian Children's Fund will feed a starving child in the third world for 80 cents a **day** (2008). In Central America and Southeast Asia, multi national corporations have opened factories to build products for export to the states. They pay from 10 to 80 cents per **hour** for child labor. One may note that private enterprise beats charity all to hell.

American labor unions whine that they are harmed by sweatshop child labor. And the leftist media will televise stories about children sold into bondage. But American imports are obviously not harming third world kids. In the third world education is a luxury. Work is a necessity.

---

[17] Reed Larson, "Stop Coddling Big Labor Thugs", Human Events, 26 Sep 97, pg. 6.

Third world workers should demand more wages or they should be denied our market, wails American labor bosses. Some young girl in the third world may starve but she must not compete. She is a scab. Competitors are scabs.

And the arrogant young, who display their insufferable ignorance and uncivil heritage by rioting on city streets and college campuses on behalf of underpaid third world competitors, are the patsies of organized labor.

The young hoods do not understand that raising wages above market in the third world will do the same as it does in the first world. It will create higher prices, wage gaps, unemployment, recession or depression, and government bailouts for the politically favored.

There are no differences in economic laws between America and the rest of the world. Any differences in economic performance are political.

Trade restrictions are not going to save the Congressional symbionts. No amount of damage control legislation is going to save organized labor and the United States Congress from the political disaster it is seeding in America.

Chapter 32

Ringworms

Wherever taxpayer's money flows in large quantities there is a growing concentration of special interests. Tax beneficiaries, from the wealthy and powerful to the indolent and lazy, accumulate about the sources of government welfare.

The many layers of government over the city require many donors to support the reelection of incumbents. Transit monopolies abound. Garbage disposal is monopolized. Utilities are monopolized. Dock workers are monopolized. Police and firemen are also. Competition is limited by permit. And grateful surwage labor donates reelection funds to incumbents.

Taxpayers flee to the suburbs. They cannot bear the tax load that the city requires to nourish the political symbionts. Politicians seek the means to curb the exodus by infringing freedom. Zoning laws and growth management acts are deployed to keep the tax base in the ringworm.

So the distances between work and home sites grow. Rush hour traffic gets worse. More taxes must be culled from outside the city or state for mass transit, for redevelopment, for public health, for welfare, and for police protection.

Vast tracts of housing lie abandoned by former owners by the squeeze of property taxes, rent control, and government mandates. What should have been a private asset becomes instead a tax load. It becomes a money loser. It can't be sold. It is abandoned by its owner.

The city seizes the property for back taxes, but politicians avoid the landlord tenant commandments that they laid on private ownership. Apartments are abandoned by their tenants as maintenance disappears. Gangs of youth and drug dealers move into abandoned units. The squalor spreads.

Everywhere in the landscape where government is injecting the taxpayer's money for the purpose of eliciting a vote or a campaign contribution, the indolent and the elitists accumulate. The blight spreads, like ringworm, under the many layers of taxing authority.

The ringworm sucks water, food, energy, and taxes from rural America and disgorges smog, garbage, sewage, and debt back into rural America.

Federal money is culled out of the larger rural landscape and piped into the ringworms. The uneven distribution of the money supply results in ringworm inflation. It is another force driving taxpayers out of the ringworms into suburbia.

It is urban sprawl, whine the dull eyed socialists who are causing the exodus.

The cities become urban islands of Democrats and their tax beneficiaries and their labor union contributors. Rural and suburban America largely represents what America was prior to the political symbiosis between ease and sleaze.

In the 2000 elections, USA Today published an issue with a map showing counties won by Gore in blue and counties won by Bush in red. The ringworms appear consistently in the blue. Had Gore carried his own state, its 11 electoral votes would have given him a win. Why did the people of Tennessee deny the presidency to a favorite son? What is the leftist news media cloaking from national view?

Crime rates in the blue landscape are about six times their rate per capita in the red landscape. Crime rates correlate well with a political spectrum that begins with those supporting seizure and redistribution of incomes on the political left and ends with those embracing the civil concepts of limited government, honesty, responsibility, and self reliance on the political right.

Chapter 33

Ringworm Fauna

As organized labor decimates the private industries it occupies, it seeks new hosts which are resistant to the seizure of surwages. Some modern targets are ringworm transportation and port facilities and their police and fire departments. They are ideal targets for the coercion of a surwage. Competition is either restricted or illegal.

On the west coast the International Longshoremen and Warehouse Union controls the docks. Average earnings are reported between 80,000 and 160,000 dollars per year.[18] The jobs are not found in want ads. An education is not required. Yet ILWU members are netting more than professionals who spend years in training. A lot more!

Their wages do not arise from public demand as honest wages must. Their wages were seized by excluding competitive labor from the docks. The ILWU is an affiliate of the Industrial Workers of the World. The preamble to the IWW Constitution grunts the following message,

---

[18] Pam Dzama, "Self-interest drives unions," The Sun, 19 Jan 03, Pg. B4.

It is the historic mission of the working class to do away with capitalism. The army of production must be organized not only for the everyday struggle with capitalists, but also to carry on production when capitalism shall have been overthrown...[19]

Note the brutish language of force (do away with, struggle, overthrown). The naked apes must think that the fruits of free enterprise blossom under the hands of hunters and gatherers. They are at war with entrepreneurs and investors who weigh the risks, gather the financial resources, and employ labor in a manner that creates a triumph of affluence over that of mere existence.

The union controls the shipping portals on the left coast of America. No imports shall cross the docks until union demands are met. Politicians will receive their kickbacks and costs will be forwarded to the consumer market. Elitist labor shall gain immensely. But millions of consumers shall lose.

In Vallejo, California the city council unanimously voted for bankruptcy. The firemen and police paid 230 and 254 dollars a month respectively to their unions to purchase a compliant city counsel. The city went broke. The average pay for firemen was 171,000 dollars per annum. A police captain received 306,000 dollars in pay and benefits.[20]

Do you know what these elites call themselves, dear reader? Millionaires!

In Washington State the Inland Boatmen's Union of the Pacific has a monopoly on cross sound ferry traffic. By the late thirties union demands had driven most ferry lines serving Puget Sound out of business. In the late forties the surviving Black Ball Line, whose wages the union controlled, and whose fares the state controlled, begged for a fare increase. The state refused. The company folded and the state bought it out. How convenient! The union gained a deep pocket for wage demands. The state promised to operate ferries only until cross sound bridges could be built. The state lied. The politicians gained a deep pocket for campaign donations.

So the freeways around Puget Sound remain crowded and a union controlled mass transit system is extolled as the solution. It is more of the same.

---

[19] Cited from website iww-org./culture/official/preamble.shtml
[20] George Will, "A City Unionized Into Bankruptcy," The Sun, 14 Sep 08, Pg. A12.

The intelligent solution is to reduce travel distances and travel times with strategically located cross sound routes. That could free up assets already in place. Tunnels and bridges do not have schedules and do not engage in strikes.

The long term solution is to end government nourishment of the ringworm and let a free people and the private sector solve the problems.

Politicians are taking much of the money generated by gas taxes and using it for mass transit (read organized labor) instead of for the driving public. Road maintenance is put off and bridges collapse. Witness the Interstate 35W bridge collapse in Minneapolis (2007). But Minnesota politicians quickly found the problem. More taxes are required.

Freeways are the greatest transportation systems ever conceived and built. Their only flaw is rush hour. And who created the rush hours? Political symbionts did it with the 8/40 work week, with zoning laws that separate homes from the workplace, and with ringworm taxes and inflation that force city workers to live in the suburbs. But tax beneficiaries, who rely on public transportation, public housing, and public welfare, will accumulate in the city. Greed overrides need when armed by law. Ringworm costs are out of control.

The construction unions collect big time in taxpayer paid Davis Bacon Act surwages wherever federal money is contributed to road construction. But roads are privately used. The Amalgamated Engineers of Shake and Bake Railways seek lifetime jobs at humongous pay in the public transit system. They will be generous with campaign funds. But roads must remain gridlocked to force ring worm fauna out of their private cars and into union operated and government owned railcars.

If industry was not captured by growth management acts or zoning law, if property taxes were low, and if full employment was the norm; industry would relocate to open spaces to lure workers with better pay, shorter commutes, and on campus employee parking.

Any labor union controlled transportation system will have horrendous operating costs. Few taxpayers will be able to use it. But they will pay for it. The tax beneficiaries will be elitist labor and politicians.

Smart cars and roads are on the horizon. The dispersal of industry into the landscape is on the horizon. The political rise of the rush hour can be rescinded. The cul-de-sac and the freeway have been marvelous in separating local and long distance traffic. The shopping mall has also. Free enterprise and affluence will solve transportation and parking problems if affluence is not destroyed by dead beat politicians.

Rails and trolleys were nice in 1900 when the alternative was ankle deep mud laced with horse manure, horse urine, and tetanus. But a century of progress has been made. The horseless carriage is here. The dispersal of industry and the demise of the rush hour are on the horizon if we make intelligent choices.

But intelligent choices cannot be made by politicians or an electorate. They can only be reached by qualified members of the private sector. There are limits to the efficacy of a democracy. A democracy is mob rule.

Chapter 34

Careers at Any Cost

Organized labor is driven by greed. Coercion does not create fair wages. It creates wage gaps. Ball players with million dollar salaries, engaging or threatening to strike, betray the union motive. One hundred million non union workers earning a politically reduced market wage of economically reduced buying power are the victims of organized labor. They should be angry. But many do not understand that unions have seized their potentially higher wages.

Strikers engage in legalized coercion. They force their demands upon others. Their surwages are the evidence. Wage gaps are the evidence. The demands and the malice exhibited at the bargaining table are the evidence. Picket line violence is the evidence. The decimation of union industry is the evidence. The taxpayer bailouts are the evidence. Recessions and depression are the evidence.

Union controlled public schools and union operated news sources have buried the coercion of surwages under bogus economic theories and inferred that unions create prosperity when they spend their gains. But they have only helped themselves by reducing the buying power of others and cheapened the dollar by pulling surwages out of production. It's a negative sum game.

The symbionts target large businesses and their customers. But the business shrinks as public demand finds alternative sources and alternative products. In the new millennium the symbionts have selected public education, public transportation, and public employment for their gains and taxpayers for their targets. Unlike consumers, the taxpayer cannot escape their grip. The symbionts know it.

The Clayton Act carried into law a rider that legalized strikes and picket lines. The bill allows the harming of the corporation and the intimidation of non union competitors seeking jobs at the wages offered. Thus we have violence occurring on the picket line and malice at the bargaining table. Wage coercion creates a continuing need for damage control legislation. One Congressional act must follow another to control the violence and prohibit business retribution. The politicians cannot break their addiction to union influence money. Damage control will continue until the final upheaval either breaks the symbiosis or ends our republic. America could become Argentina north.

In 1973 the Supreme Court placed labor bosses beyond the reach of federal prosecutors enforcing the Hobbs Anti Extortion Act. But the court illuminated the distinction between extortion and coercion. The distinction is legal. There is no economic distinction.

Many cars on American roads are foreign models. Most ships in American ports are foreign made and foreign operated. Most manufactured goods sold in America are foreign made. Soon most aircraft visiting American airports will be foreign made.

Labor unions are shrinking America's industrial foundation. They dumb down American education. Their political interference with free trade angers other nations. They weakened American industry in the thirties and invited war in the forties. How long will we tolerate this economic insanity?

Coercing surwages on a grand scale has global consequences. Wage gaps widen. Minimum wage laws are required for damage control. The wage shortage grows. A recession follows. Inflation of the money supply is required to counter unemployment. Then a negative balance of trade follows.

Our trading partners buy up American businesses with their excess Federal Reserve Notes. Soon we will have nothing left to sell. Foreign trade will end. And the Congressional symbionts will give the people the mother of all economic collapses. The Great Depression was not enough. And the Congress will once again blame private enterprise. How long are the American people going to buy into colossal Congressional lies?

But in the United States Congress the puppets of labor are helpless. They dance on the strings of organized labor for campaign contributions. And they pursue Congressional careers at any cost to the public or to the republic.

Oh what tangled webs we weave when first we practice to deceive.

Part v.
The Wages of Sin

The Great Depression should have ended the economic farce of raising wages by law. But the Congress and the media did a number on private enterprise. Private enterprise received blame for the economic disaster. The Congress, in its endless search for campaign funds, had enacted the conditions for a depression over many years. And they escaped responsibility for both creating the depression and sustaining it for over a decade.

Americans not only lost prosperity but our economic decline greatly harmed our credibility on the world stage. We invited war upon ourselves.

Chapter 35

Prelude to a Depression

Imagine a society of twenty people and an aggregate wage flow of 100,000 dollars per annum among workers. This flow might be divided into 5000 dollars per annum to all workers or 10,000 dollars per annum to half of all workers. What is this society's better choice?

The wise society will choose to let wages fall until all workers are employed. Twenty employed people will produce twice as much as will ten. Their aggregate production will be doubled.

But socialists would demand the greater wage. By hogging the wage flow, they halve employment and halve production. The ten in the half employed society can live as well as the twenty in the fully employed society, but only if the unemployed are banished. Society cannot gain by the redistribution of wages.

But society can lose. If the ten employed engage in perfect socialist sharing with the ten unemployed, they will share half of the standard of living they could share in the fully employed society. The labor of ten will produce half as much to share as the labor of twenty. The buying power of their wage is half of what it could be. Buying power arises out of employment and production.

The wise society will allow the natural competition for jobs to limit wages rather than allow the political coercion of wages to limit jobs.

The wise society will recognize the unproductive nature of surwages and outlaw labor strikes. The seizure of wages by collective is economically no different than theft by individuals, except that it harms far more victims. And full employment would put unskilled labor in a sellers market (where it normally would be) and naturally raise minimum wages.

The inverse relationship between wage rates and employment cannot be voided by law. The Great Depression is presented next. The reader is prepared to understand it.

Chapter 36

The Great Depression

The great depression was a product of a labor union influenced Congress. No one will learn of this in their labor union controlled and government funded school. The great labor catastrophe will be sanitized.

The first thing one need know is that a recession or a depression is characterized by massive unemployment. The other thing one need know is that unemployment is a political euphemism for a labor surplus. Labor is a commodity. And every manager in America knows how to clear a surplus of any commodity. You lower its price.

And it is not minimum wages that need to be lowered. Minimum wages were never determined by employer greed. They were determined by the greed of organized labor. Employers do not cause wage shortages or their alternative, wage gaps. Elitist labor does. When a labor surplus occurs, it is overpriced labor that needs to be put on sale.

Overpriced labor would normally lower their demands to maintain their employment, but politically overpriced labor does not have to. They are armed by law.

The congressional symbiosis with labor created the great economic disaster. The Federal Reserve also played a role. The feds can readily reduce the nation's money supply by increasing the cost of credit. But increasing the money supply by reducing the cost of credit is much more difficult. People will not borrow when their ability to pay their debts is threatened by job losses.

The Federal Reserve lost control when the demand for loans plummeted with the stock market in 1929. They watched the nation's money supply collapse along with the nation's aggregate wage.

But if the money supply falls, wage rates <u>or</u> employment must also fall. But wage rates were supported by labor legislation. Employment must fall instead. Remember that hourly wage rates and man hours of employment are always inversely related by a finite money supply.

The Congress continued to bash the economy throughout the thirties with legislation designed to raise wage rates. It is more of the same! The Congress sustained and prolonged the depression.

The great farce began in 1913. The Federal Reserve System was created in 1913. The Clayton Act, which legalized strikes and job site picketing, was enacted in 1914. The framework for a depression was laid.

The Federal Reserve Act created a fractional reserve banking system. Bankers could profit by loaning money normally reserved for demand accounts. More significantly, the reserve multiplier was born. The feds could expand the money supply. They failed to appreciate that it could also contract.

The natural tendency of market prices is to fall as productivity rises. Retailers will lower prices until they sell. The natural tendency of wages also is to fall as employment rises. Workers will lower their wage demands until they are hired.

Lower prices mark the fruits of more efficient producers. Consumers are attracted to better buys. The less competitive must lower costs to survive. They might lower their labor costs, but they cannot lower wages below market. At that point their labor can walk to market wage jobs opening elsewhere. And that is where the natural balance begins.

Unfair wails the politician and labor union symbionts. Union labor is the least efficient and most costly of any class of labor. Coercion has set their wages far above their market worth. Union organized industry is avoided by market demand. The natural market is expected to blindly pay the surwage. But the market is not insensitive to plunder. Higher prices lower demand. There is no market demand for overpriced labor. Their never has been. There never can be.

A fair wage is always paid if labor is free to quit (not enslaved). But a surwage must be coerced by threat of a strike and competitive labor intimidated by threat of assault.

The Congress and their labor union campaign contributors enter into a political symbiosis. Laws will be made. Magic will prevail. Wages shall be raised by law.

While organized labor was coercing their wage rates upward in the twenties, the Federal Reserve System embarked on monetary expansion. It simply means increasing the money supply by increasing the authority of member banks to loan. An expanding money supply raises demand. More money is bid for the aggregate national product. Inflation begins.

Inflation raises corporate income. Wage rates (but not buying power) and employment are both free to rise as the money supply infusing corporate America rises. But labor had gained political power from the Congress with the Clayton Act. The industrial labor unions will plunder the growing money supply due to monetary expansion in the twenties. They will coerce a disproportionate share of the growing aggregate wage for themselves.

Politically caused wage gaps make their first appearance in the ranks of unskilled labor in the twenties. The wage spectrum is widened between low paid retail and farm labor and high paid industrial labor as the aggregate wage expands. In 1929 Hoover created the Farm Board to raise farm incomes. One corrupt act begets another. Damage control never ends.

Murray Rothbard writes that the feds expanded the money supply in response to British inflation.[21] The British economy in the twenties was suffering the effects of trade unionism compounded by generous unemployment benefits. Strikes were rife in the British landscape. British labor unions were coercing their way to wealth. But their production was not following their wages. They were buying their wealth offshore.

British gold was flowing to the US to redeem British paper. The US retained a gold standard (until 1934). The Federal Reserve engaged in monetary inflation to ameliorate the British gold loss. Their alibi was to save the international gold standard. An alibi is a sham reason for a covert real reason.

To cooperate in international inflation, it is necessary to augment gold certificates with Federal Reserve notes. Federal Reserve notes are not

---

[21] Murray Rothbard, "America's Great Depression," fourth edition, Richardson and Snyder, 1983, pg. 131.

certificates of title to specific ounces of gold or silver coin. They are the governmental equivalent of an IOU. But they are legal tender. If two governments were to counterfeit equally, then the gold flow between their countries could be minimized. They could exchange IOUs. A gold loss might be averted.

However, their citizens will suffer inflation as the money supply expands.

Two might play the game. Too many, will not agree on how much money to counterfeit. Wars, organized labor, and politics set corrupt governments on separate economic courses and unevenly cheapen their national currencies. The gold standard must eventually succumb to variable exchange rates.

Let us return to the twenties. Monetary expansion in America had not only augmented a growing wage gap between union and non union workers, it had also inflated the capital market. The value of corporate stocks soared.

It is instructive to ponder the total value of stock in the stock market in a free and natural economy. Would the total value of all stock increase over time? The aggregate real value of all stock in corporate America must increase as the nation's economy and infrastructure expand. But as production expands, the buying power of the dollar expands also. The value of the dollar increases. Therefore a broad index of stocks, measured in dollars of appreciating worth could rise only with real economic growth.

But something new was happening in the twenties. Monetary expansion was depreciating the dollar and inflating the stock market. In prior experience winners were often balanced by losers. But after 1913 (and fractional reserve banking), it appeared that winners far outnumbered the losers. A broad portfolio of stocks looked like a safe and profitable haven for mattress money.

The market was soaring. The stock market was drawing money normally invested in savings in the banking system. Political pressure was building to slap down the stock market. That pressure no doubt came from the banking industry.

Each of twelve Federal Reserve banks is a corporation. Member banks are stockholders in their corporation. Their stock cannot be traded publicly.

They are locked into a small annual dividend set by law.[22] And stock market returns were outperforming the returns on bank savings. Did the federal banking system decide to bring their competition in the private stock market down, by ending monetary expansion?

Believe me! Politics is all about bashing competitors. In the year 2000 the feds brought the private stock market to its knees by again ending monetary expansion. They justified their self serving action with a great political alibi and a relatively new federal euphemism called an overheated economy. The real reason for their egregious action will be revealed in Part VII.

Monetary expansion ended in December of 1928. There is a delay between market insult and market response. The stock market began its deflation on 24 October 1929. Then the feds totally lost control.

Fractional reserve banking allows small increases in excess reserves to multiply many more times. It is called the reserve multiplier. After the market crash, U.S. banks prudently restricted their loans and used their funds to pay back Federal Reserve loans. By the second quarter of 1932 the banks were increasing their reserves beyond the legal minimum. The multiplier became a divider. The money decline once put in motion had assumed a life of its own. The feds had lost control of the money supply.

In the thirties corporate America lost income as the money supply collapsed. The stock market suffered continuous deflation. But organized labor will not give up their surwages. High wages are necessary to maintain consumer demand the symbionts whine.

But wage rates must fall in step with the contraction of corporate income or employment cannot be sustained. It is employment and production that should be sustained and not the surwages of labor. Remove the political obstacles. Let wages fall. Prices will follow. Deflation will end (as will unemployment) when wages and prices find their balance with the politically dithered money supply.

The aggregate number of jobs that could be sustained by corporate America was sharply reduced from 1929 to 1934 as government taxed and converted potentially lower private wages into generous public wages. The construction of Hoover dam was an example. But the inverse relation between wage

---

[22] It is 6% today.

rates and employment prevailed. The symbionts further hogged the wage supply.

In their book, The Hoover Administration, Myers and Newton provide extracts from some Hoover speeches delivered during the 1932 presidential campaign. The speeches are remarkable in that they reveal the problem, but without recognition.

> **We might have done nothing. That would have been utter ruin. Instead we met the situation with proposals to private business and the Congress of the most gigantic program of economic defense and counterattack ever evolved in the history of the Republic. We put it into action.**[23]

> **At the outset of the depression we brought about an understanding between employers and employees that wages should be maintained. They were maintained until the cost of living had decreased and the profits had practically vanished. They are now <u>the highest real wages in the world</u>.**[24]

Wonderful! The unemployed must have been thrilled to hear that.

> **No government in Washington has hitherto considered that it held so broad a responsibility for leadership in such times...For the first time in the history of depression, dividends, profits, and the cost of living have been reduced before wages have suffered...**[25]

The great economic warrior actually reveals the problem in his insistence that wages do not fall. But he does not recognize it. He does not know that wage rates and employment are inversely related by a finite money supply.

Roosevelt did not recognize the inverse relation either.

---

[23] Cited from "The Hoover Administration," by William Starr Myers and Walter H. Newton, Republished by Scholarly Press, Inc., 1977, Pg 249.
[24] Ibid, Pg. 251.
[25] Ibid, Pg. 250.

Hoover admits to unprecedented government interference with the natural setting of wages in his speeches. Yet he cannot imagine unemployment problems arising as the result of unprecedented government interference with the natural setting of wages. He seems oblivious to the universal law of cause and effect.

But politicians can never admit to misfeasance. Their political careers come first. Politicians must always fault private enterprise for economic tragedies. And need we wonder why socialist morons hate private enterprise?

The Supreme Court's corrupt upholding of the National Labor Relations Act of 1935 led to further wage coercion. The natural balance between the buyer and seller of labor was biased further toward labor. Wages jumped 13.7 percent in the first three quarters of 1937 bringing about a sharp decline in employment in late 1937. Wonderful!

Unemployment was still in double digits when World War II brought about a market recovery. Thus some socialist morons believe that free enterprise can only prosper on war or other Keynesian government spending.

But the private sector is not free. The economy revived when government started buying war goods. Taxpayers and war bonds paid the industrial surwages that consumer demand evaded. The political power to strike was curtailed as the probability of war loomed. Unemployment fell as labor was drafted into military service and wages were lowered and spread. It could have been consumer goods in lieu of war goods. Laws allowing the hoarding of wages by organized labor need only have been rescinded.

In 1929 the Congress should have removed 16 years of socialist labor legislation. They should have outlawed strikes and allowed wages to seek market value. Private enterprise would have quickly restored the job market.

To be candid, the thirties Congress could not fix the economic problem. They would not challenge the hogging of wages by organized labor. They would not sacrifice their careers. They can only attempt to override the damage.

Free enterprise lowers wages **and** prices until all workers are hired and all products are sold. Set enterprise free. Then leave it alone. It is self balancing. It balances at maximum productivity and affluence.

But labor gained much political power in the socialist years. In 1914 there was the Clayton Act. In 1926 there was the Railway Labor Act. In 1930 there was the Smoot Hawley Act. In 1931 there was the Davis-Bacon Act. In 1932 there was the Norris-La Guardia Act. And in 1932 the socialist morons doubled federal tax rates. They pulled more potential wages out of the economic landscape.

In 1935 the egregious National Labor Relations Act seeped out of the House of Bribes. And in 1938 the Fair Labor Standards Act was dropped into the devastated economic landscape. Herein lay the roots of the depression. The economy was taking hit after hit from the socialist morons. Why do morons insist on fixing something they cannot understand?

The Congress raised taxes to fund myriads of farm and family relief acts. It is all damage control. Potential wages were pulled out of the landscape with new taxes. Union power to hog wages should have been removed. Employers should have been encouraged to lower their wages and prices (as they normally would do in free enterprise) to increase sales and jobs toward their optimum. The market could have restored employment in the least amount of time if not prohibited by law. The political prohibitions should have been rescinded.

Twenty eight percent of the workforce was unemployed by 1934. Isn't it time to quench labor violence by eliminating its motivation, wage gaps and unemployment? Isn't it time to end the surwage instead of financing unemployment, retarding economic growth, cheapening the dollar, expanding the wage gaps, and suffering the political destruction of free enterprise?

After the war, strikes and inflation raged in the economic landscape. The Taft-Hartley Act reduced union political power and stemmed a return to the depression. But the wage gaps remained in the economic landscape and the Republican Congress paid dearly for passing the act over Truman's veto.

Attempts to curb special interests are often political suicide. Damage control is the preferred course. And an ignorant electorate is in deep trouble.

The depression reached into several democracies in the western world to the extent that organized labor in their countries was empowered by law to seize surwages. Some writers have faulted bank failures somewhere for initiating the depression. Banking failures will normally create an economic transient of limited reach and finite duration. But any disturbance can bring down a house of cards. It takes political wage supports to surplus labor when the money supply declines or when economic velocity declines.

Industry, burdened with surwage costs, continues to evaporate in America and condense in more honest labor environments in Japan, Taiwan, South Korea, Indonesia, and in the new millennium, China. It does not condense in Marxist Europe where labor unions prevail and double digit unemployment reigns.

During the Carter administration, Americans endured **stagflation**. The political symbionts were pulling the average wage rate up for the politically favored and the surwages were removed from the potential employment and production of others. Production fell. And the feds seriously inflated the money supply. The double whammy produced double digit inflation.

Inflation funded the surwages of labor. But wage gaps were widened and unemployment continued. We moved in the direction of the half employed society the author imagined in Prelude to a Depression.

Reagan's income tax cut circa 1982 cleared the growing labor surplus by increasing disposable income and lowering consumer costs. In Part VI the author will show how marginal taxes on personal income can be shifted to the consumer by the invisible hand of supply and demand.

And Reagan fought the surwage. He fired air traffic controllers when their monopoly went on strike.

Here are some dark thoughts. Was saving the gold standard simply a political alibi for expanding the money supply in the twenties? Did the feds anticipate and attempt to counter unemployment by expanding the wage supply? Did British and American banking authorities collude to expand the aggregate wage in their economic landscapes to offset the surwages of organized labor in their corrupt political landscapes?

But the symbiosis of Marxist greed and Congressional careers is too strong. Surwages rise to counter monetary inflation. The feds and the congressional symbionts initiate a wage price spiral. Politically disfavored labor is left struggling in the wake. And the wage gaps grow.

A labor surplus can occur but momentarily in a free market. The coercion of surwages must end. Strikes must be prohibited. Strikers must forfeit their jobs by law. The surwage must be outlawed.

Balance begins with an employer paying what he must to lure employees away from other jobs in a fully employed society and with the employee seeking work at the best wages he can find. This is the quintessential means of balancing wages (and consequently prices) with the money supply.

<u>Damn few people earn minimum wages</u>. It is self evident that a wage floor is not required to support wages. But a ceiling needs to be placed on incomes seized under color of law. Minimum wages would naturally soar if unearned wages were not being seized at the high end of the scale.

Remarkably the balance arises between individuals at the grass roots level. Political attempts to raise wages by law are absurd. They destroy a natural balance, cause a maldistribution of income, initiate unemployment, and invite government zeroes to initiate yet greater economic disaster.

Economics must be a part of a civil education. That means that our schools must be taken out of the hands of the education unions and the political brainwash ended. The natural inverse relationship between wage rates and employment should be common knowledge. The direct relationship between honest employment and buying power should be common knowledge. And the political expansion of wage gaps should be economic history and manifestly prohibited.

One wonders, are we civil enough to embrace the prime rule of civilization?

Thou shall not steal.

Meatballs

Many years ago there was a radio commercial advertising Mug root beer. As a service to listeners the ad explained how to train your pet lobo wolf. Basically one gives the predator a command and lobs it a meatball. This procedure is to be repeated forever. The last instruction emphasized, <u>do not</u> run out of meatballs.

Franklin Roosevelt backpedaled from predatory labor during the depression. Big labor was out of control. The Congress had created a monster. And the monster had spawned huge wage gaps and unemployment (the ultimate wage gap). The predators blamed robber barons and private enterprise for the disaster. Neither Roosevelt nor his political party will override big labor. Labor unions are their life support system. They remain so today.

Instead he warred with the Axis powers. The war gave him the political alibi he needed to quench wage demands. Rationing curbed consumer demands and controlled prices. War bonds funded new wages and war jobs. And many of the unemployed found room and board in the military.

The Congress has been lobbing meatballs to labor unions and the politically connected for nearly a century. Eventually, the taxpayers will be impoverished and our treacherous Congress will run out of meatballs.

But will the public recognize the Congress as the source of the economic disaster? Or will they wrongly fault private enterprise and seek out the very perpetrator of their ills for their salvation? Like some dumb lovesick battered wife? They did so in the thirties.

Chapter 38

The Moron and the Weed

Once upon a time there was a moron. He didn't realize he was a moron of course. He had been ejoocated in public skools by organized labor. The moron assumed responsibility for maintaining a beautiful public garden that resided in a natural balance with its environment.

Then one day the moron discovered a weed. This is not allowable. Something must be done. The moron decides to drown the weed. "I will apply copious amounts of water to this weed," he declares. He waters it for an hour.

The next day the weed has grown. This is not allowable. The moron declares war on the weed. "I will mount the most gigantic program of defense and counterattack in the history of the republic," he declares. He brings to bear yet more garden hoses for drowning the weed, for yet more hours.

The next day the weed has grown. This is not allowable. The moron assumes leadership. "No gardener in Washington has hitherto considered that he held so broad a responsibility for leadership in such times," he declares. He brings to bear a fire hose from a street hydrant to drown the weed. The water pressure feeding other flowers in the garden begins to drop.

The next day the weed has grown. This is not allowable. More must be done. "Nothing has ever been devised in our history which has done more for the common run of men and women," he declares. He brings yet more fire hoses to bear on the weed. The water pressure feeding other flowers in the garden drops precipitously.

The next day the weed has grown. It is now the largest weed in the history of weeds. But the flowers are dying.

An intelligent person would have questioned whether what he was doing was harmful long before the flowers died en masse. That is why we call our hero a moron.

Are politicians morons? Or are they merely puppets of organized labor?

Two decades of government-labor union mucking in the natural economy to raise wages for some above the market supply of wages came to an economically predictable result, an unprecedented labor surplus.

Elected officials cannot admit to misfeasance, malfeasance, nonfeasance, or bribery. Since there are only two players in the economics game, politicians have to blame all economic problems on the other player, private enterprise.

Politicians are always innocent.

Chapter 39

The Sleeping Giant

After the Japanese attack on Pearl Harbor, Admiral Yamamoto is reputed to have expressed a fear that they had only awakened a sleeping giant and filled him with a fierce resolve. He may have recognized a potential in America that his peers could not. He had been in America.

The great depression made it appear as if America was fading from the world stage in the thirties. The depression dragged on. Industrial output had fallen by one third. Quiet steel mills were rusting. Food lines were common. Millions were homeless.

Japanese industrial output was growing during the same period. Why should they not think that the American century was over and that the Japanese century was in ascent?

Japan had never suffered from Marxist labor unionism. How could they recognize the strangle hold that a corrupt Congress and organized labor held on the United States economy?

With war came economic demand in the form of war material purchases. The Japanese had mistaken a politically poisoned American economy for impotence. They grabbed a tiger by the tail. The economy roared to life.

The depression had reduced their perceived risk of losing a war with the United States. But did the depression also steer American foreign policy into a war as a political means to sidestep labor and restore economic demand? Roosevelt and his inner circle knew. But we can only surmise.

O what tangled webs we weave when first we practice to deceive.

Part vi

Great Lies and Taxes

If a tax increase laid on the seller of a product causes the market price of the product to increase, the tax has wholly or in part been shifted from the seller to the buyer. The buyer becomes a tax payer. The seller becomes a tax collector. Taxes that do this include graduated income taxes, sin taxes, and corporate taxes of all kinds.

But graduated income taxes have a split personality. They fall on a wide spectrum of labor. The invisible hand of supply and demand will readily transfer taxes on those in high market demand to the consumer. This unintended consequence occurs because public demand for professionals will create the <u>net</u> incomes necessary to attract the capable into professional careers. <u>Gross</u> incomes (their net income plus their income taxes) affect only their costs to consumers.

Thus the graduated tax is the most regressive tax in the economic landscape. Unskilled labor will pay their lower bracket taxes as wage earners and assume the higher bracket taxes of professionals as consumers.

Part VI reveals the stealthy nature of taxes and politicians who champion them.

Chapter 40

The Graduated Income Tax

The graduated income tax has to be the most destructive tax ever conceived by human greed. And it is a costly nightmare to implement and enforce. But it maximizes government seizure and it does so in a manner few will understand.

There is a common belief that high earners pay a much greater proportion of their income in taxes than does the little guy. But economic forces override politics. It certainly appears that high earners are targeted when one reads the statistics published by the Internal Revenue Service. But the statistics only illuminate the **apparent** tax payers. They never illuminate consumers. They never reveal how taxes on <u>market set</u> income are passed to the point of sale.

The natural economy is remarkable for advancing the presence of professionally and technically trained people for the betterment of mankind. The profit motive lures capable people into the necessary education and training. But the graduated income tax maliciously seeks to enslave the labor of the capable into Marxian servitude to others. It fails its purpose.

Public attention is focused on gross incomes. But that is not where the action is. The natural mix of labor talent in the economic landscape is normally determined by <u>net</u> incomes.

To illuminate how supply and demand can readily shift personal income taxes from those targeted to the consumer, we may assume that an economy in quiet equilibrium is suddenly unbalanced by a change in tax rates and we may deduce the market response over time.

Assume that socialists in the Congress have just created havoc in the economic landscape by raising the marginal income tax rate from 50 percent to 75 percent. We can further limit our analysis to the income of medical doctors and assume for clarity that all doctors are in the same marginal income tax bracket. What happens?

Economics happens!

Doctors see their net income suddenly cut in half. It drops from 50 percent of their gross income to 25 percent of their gross income. Many doctors will immediately retire.

The worthy doctor had plans to practice another 5 years, retire, purchase a suitable sailing vessel, and sail around the globe. He now sees perhaps 10 years to do so and he will have 5 years less of his remaining life to enjoy his dream. He won't take the gamble. He will immediately retire and scale back his retirement plans. He won't work for half pay.

The doctor's 18 year old son is in the freshman class. He is working, but not earning. He faces a decade or more of medical training before he can even begin to pay back the indebtedness that training will accrue. Now his potential return has been halved and his payback period doubled. He may not live that long. He detests state enslavement and he can recognize it. He will enter the work force earlier and accumulate his wealth over a longer, if lesser, career.

This story in its many variations will take place on a grand scale. The supply of doctors in the economic landscape will immediately begin to contract as an initial result of new marginal taxes on their income.

But as the numbers of doctors dwindle the number of patients seen by the remaining doctors must increase. Therefore the gross incomes of doctors will rise.

But their fees will rise also. Doctors must hire staff to handle the load. Patients who can ill afford to wait for an opening in the doctor's calendar will pay the necessary fees. The **supply** of doctors will fall and the **demand** for their services will rise. They are the unavoidable economic effects of the tax increase.

Taxes cannot be raised without a market response.

But society regresses. There are fewer doctors and they charge more. Their visits with patients are shorter. The waiting lines are longer. Unfortunately, damn few people will recognize a lack of doctors and their wait for medical services as the unintended consequence of a tax assault on higher incomes.

Doctors cannot be enslaved in the free society. Their numbers will dwindle. Patient care will deteriorate. Some of the ill must pay with their lives. And lawsuits will only deter more potential doctors from pursuing a medical career and further drive up the cost and the wait for medical care.

Net income affects the supply of doctors. Gross income affects only their costs to consumers. The dichotomy between gross and net earnings represents a fundamental economic flaw in the Marxist tax. The number of doctors will stop dwindling when their net income again entices enough youth into the profession to replace those leaving.

Prior to the increase in the marginal tax rate, a doctor collected a dollar for the IRS and a dollar for himself. After the tax increase and market readjustment, a doctor collects three dollars for the IRS and a dollar for himself. The doctor, like the corporation, is collecting taxes from consumers for the government.

Sure, doctors and potential doctors took an initial bashing. But after the medical profession shrinks and the market finds its new balance, the consumer then takes the bashing (as he does following corporate bashings).

Doctors are also consumers. They will pay the tax to other providers out of their net income, like everyone else. But the doctor's net income will have returned to market value. Market value is where the doctors net income was initially, and to where it must return before the medical profession will cease its shrinkage.

This superb natural economic readjustment keeps the medical profession from dwindling to zero. It remains in the economic landscape albeit smaller. The adjustment is made by millions of buyers and sellers acting only in the aggregate. Government does not possess aggregate knowledge. A million unneeded federally hired drones could not replace the finesse of millions of consumers pursuing their own interests in free enterprise. When government targets any group for state slavery, it reduces their presence in the workforce.

Review the mechanics of the tax shift. A rise in doctor fees (gross income) will lower consumer <u>demand</u> for doctors by very little. Illness sets the demand. But a drop in the professions net income will lower the <u>supply</u> of doctors by a lot. Both demand and supply will fall. But the ensuing rise in the demand to supply ratio (patients to doctors) will initiate a natural rise in the income of doctors remaining. If the rise in net incomes offsets the initial drop in net incomes from the tax increase, then consumers have assumed the doctors' marginal tax increase. And that is exactly what happens wherever there is inelastic market demand for a class of labor.

IRS figures for the year 2000 claim that the top 10 percent of earners (income above $92,100) pay 67 percent of income taxes. But the figures are grossly misleading. They do not reveal the history of changes in earned income that are brought about by marginal tax increases and supply and demand. In income tax revenue statistics, consumers are never counted as taxpayers, and the apparent taxpayers are never discounted as tax collectors.

We can reasonably conclude that <u>two thirds</u> (perhaps more) of income tax revenue is collected from consumers by market demand, because the top ten percent of earners are obviously in market demand.

It is certainly nice to be in the entertainment business. Michael Jackson could entertain his fans by the thousands in one performance. The less fortunate doctor must entertain his customers one at a time. But in either case, the demand to supply ratio determines the earning power of the individual.

On the other hand, the natural market will pay <u>no more than necessary</u> to affect a balance. A marginal tax break for the doctor would quickly be reflected in lower consumer costs and more practitioners. Nothing can replace the aggregate finesse of supply and demand. Politicians can only create a shortage of professionals and raise the costs for their services. That is what the socialist morons do. But there is another revelation.

Progressive taxes on earned income can not be sustained in free enterprise. Free men will avoid attempts to enslave their labor.

There is a natural wage distribution set by the market value of the individual. Overlying the natural distribution is a government imposed and a progressively widening marginal tax rate. The gross sum of market set net incomes and government set marginal taxes makes ten percent of earners appear to be scalpers. But it is only the government that is engaged in scalping and only the consumer who is being scalped.

The marginal income tax appears to be progressive when viewed from the gross income it is calculated on. But marginal incomes tend to rise in step with marginal tax increases. It does so to restore the <u>net</u> incomes of those in market demand. Since it is inelastic consumer demand that boosts marginal incomes in the first place, one should not be surprised that consumers pay for the marginal widening.

Mother Nature is just not fair. The harder the socialist morons try to kick high earners in the butt, the more their asses hurt.

Interestingly enough, the invisible hand of supply and demand will not shift a marginal tax increase on the surwages of organized labor to the market. Surwages are not determined by supply and demand. They are seized by force of law. A rise in the marginal tax rate will eat up the <u>unearned</u> surwages of organized labor.

A free economy is a marvelous natural engine for promoting earned incomes and thwarting unearned incomes. Natural competition, if not thwarted by law, might provide all the regulatory mechanisms necessary in a free business world. Economic disasters emanate from government. Politicians are not needed.

Abolishment of the income tax would abruptly reverse market forces. The number of professionals in the landscape would rise, lured there by the increase in net pay. Health care would become abundant. There would be no tax burden passed to patients. The costs for medical services would fall. Insurance costs would fall. The patient's income could be his gross earnings. Supply could lead demand in removing the economic damage. Doctors might make house calls. Patients might afford them.

Can consumers avoid the transfer of marginal taxes on earned higher incomes to the market? Sure. They could avoid the products or services of professionals. They could live and die like a primitive. The tax on marginal incomes causes the natural mix of labor in the economic landscape to regress and the ranks of the unskilled to increase.

Wonderful!

But taxes on your labor were not enough. The Sixteenth Amendment conveniently addresses income instead of earnings. The graduated income tax has found its success in seizing the citizen's good fortune, his surwage, or his inheritance. But it cannot reach <u>earned</u> higher income. A free people will avoid servitude.

Chapter 41

Corporate Taxes

Anyone who has had their car repaired will receive a bill that itemizes material and labor plus a sales tax. The buyer will pay the total. The seller will collect the sales tax for the government.

But what is a material cost? As we follow production back through corporate America from end products toward their sources, we find that material costs arise, at each step in the climb to retail level, from labor and government costs. At the source, matter and energy are provided gratis by Mother Nature. And at retail, material or energy costs are simply an aggregate sum of wages and taxes.

Labor charges are also an aggregate sum of various labor and government costs. Your auto mechanic will not receive the 100 dollars per hour labor charge. The labor charge will bundle taxes, fees, licenses, permits, insurance, utilities, and legal costs on a per hour basis and forward them to the point of sale.

The market price at the point of sale is always a sum of labor and taxes. All costs are forwarded to consumers. If they cannot be forwarded, the supplier enters bankruptcy. Governments can never realize the taxes they reach for. But economic zeroes in government will continue to reach.

Now we may talk of corporate America's income arising out of corporate sales and being broadly distributed as income to the private sector and as taxes to government (federal, state, local). And we can clarify the economic roles of wage earners and government.

It should be clear that corporate America does not pay taxes. It is the consumer that carries the tax burden. The corporation is merely a tax collector. Any tax lusting politician that says that corporations must pay more taxes is either a damn fool or he takes his listeners for fools. Your call!

Now we add the compliance costs of federal mandates. That is another bundle. Compliance costs lengthen the manufacturing process. They result in more labor and tax expenses to pass to market.

Hidden taxes are said to constitute about 8 percent of the retail price.[26] This is a remarkably low estimate. It surely does not include two thirds of all income tax revenues that are transferred to consumers by supply and demand. The reader already knows how that occurs.

And now you pay the one tax that is visible to most consumers. You pay a sales tax. It is merely a decoy. It is merely the tip of the iceberg.

Government will cost you more than anything else in your life. And it will cost you your freedom if not your life. Your federal government is **out of control**.

Chapter 42

Grandma and Grandpa are Burdens

Taxes on income have created the **do it yourself** revolution. The graduated income tax has led us to evade income taxes. We do it for ourselves. We have become plumbers, carpenters, electricians, and painters in our spare time. Most of us would prefer to hire help. But our own labor is tax free. Hired labor has all kinds of taxes embedded in it.

In Asian countries, where Marxism has not penetrated and income is not taxed, many citizens can afford domestic servants. Asian families can also take care of their aged. Most American families can do neither.

---

[26] "NTUF Study Exposes $639 Billion in Hidden Taxes", Capital Ideas, National Taxpayers Union Foundation, vol. 6, no. 2, summer 1998.

Because of labor laws one must hire six people to cover a 24/7 work week or pay many hours of overtime for hiring fewer. And one must pay minimum wage rates 24/7. Taxes on labor and labor law allow only the very wealthy to provide live in home care for grandma or grandpa.

Many Americans must place their aging parent(s) in a nursing home. They have no choice. The gross pay of hired help greatly exceeds the net earnings of those who would hire them. Many of the elderly victims, torn from their families by labor law and taxes on income, will become taxpayer burdens. And their children's potential inheritance will be seized by the state to pay for the federally enacted social catastrophe.

Ain't guvmint wonderful?

Why not repeal labor laws? Leftoids in the political establishment love their 24/7 labor rules. Labor laws illuminate home maintenance and home care for taxing and amplify income tax revenues.

To a revenue lusting political overlord, overtime means overtax.

Chapter 43

The Ability to Pay

Tax the ability to pay, grunt the naked apes on the political left. At least they recognize the impossible. Government cannot seize taxes where there is no ability to pay.

Economic zeroes support a graduated income tax because they think someone else is paying. They do not know that two thirds of income taxes (taxes in the higher brackets) are shifted to consumers by inelastic market demand.

But there is another tax scheme based on an ability to pay that is forcing people to flee the slave states. It is forcing them to abandon their homes that they established during their working lives. It is property taxes.

In Washington State a state income tax is unconstitutional. But the leftist legislature found a way to foist an income tax on the people anyway.

In Washington one can qualify for a property tax break if his retirement income is such that he can hardly afford to keep his overtaxed home. He will not have to pay that which he cannot pay. He gets to live in his home (if only in poverty). It is a gift from his benevolent legislature and their fairness charade. One gets the same fairness when he cooperates with the armed robber. He gets to live.

If politicians were to start a mass eviction of taxpayers from their homes because of outrageous property taxes, they would be facing a political rebellion. Taxing on the ability to pay is not a fairness doctrine. It is merely a gunfire avoidance tactic. It is a method to coerce the greatest amount of taxes out of the people without provoking a violent response.

Somewhat the same technique is used by the master in breaking a slave or training a dog.

Chapter 44

Capital Gains

Everything ages over time. So do the homes of taxpayers. So how can one sell their home of thirty years for more than they paid for it? They don't. It just appears so.

It takes a dollar to buy what a dime would buy years before. Your sale is proof. But there is no gain. A new home similar to the old would cost you much more. But political liars will claim your house gained value by aging. They will have their hand in your pocket to collect a capital gains tax when you sell.

But monetary expansion has merely cheapened the buying power of the dollar. That is why more dollars are required to purchase a home that has merely aged. The federal government first steps on you with inflationary policy (printing more and more money) and then penalizes you for getting stepped on.

A person can buy an acre in the country and be encircled over many years by ringworm growth. The value of his property may be enhanced if his surroundings are improved. But what most properties gain in surroundings will be lost in depreciation, property taxes, ringworm taxes, and ringworm inflation. There is no net gain.

With the exceptions of some fine wines, artwork, or corporate stock, an alleged capital gain is nothing but inflation. It is another great lie and tax scam perpetrated by your federal government. Inflation makes this tax lucrative for politicians. This tax would be impotent if not for government counterfeiting of the money supply.

Chapter 45

Sharing Your Burden

Let us suppose it is an election year and benevolent state politicians are out to do the taxpayer a favor. They want to relieve the taxpayer of half of his burden.

Sure!

The state is going to cut the state sales tax in half, from 8 percent to 4 percent. To make up for the government shortfall, the politicians propose that the retailers match your tax contribution with an equal tax contribution. You will pay a 4 percent tax on all purchases. The retailer will pay a 4 percent tax on all sales. Can you believe this?

The retailer gets all his revenue from corporate sales. Corporate income is disbursed for wholesale purchases, for the wages of labor, for facilities and utilities, and for numerous other taxes, licenses, and permits. How will the corporation pay the new tax burden?

If wages are one half of corporate expense, wages must be cut by 8 percent to offset a 4 percent tax loss on sales. And wages, if set by supply and demand, cannot be cut. Neither can profit. Profit margins can be less than tax margins. And profit separates success from bankruptcy. If wages and profits are sacrosanct, then prices must be raised to finance the new tax. The retailer can only adjust his wages, his prices, and his profit margin. He cannot control external costs.

There will be no hand wringing by management on what must be done. A price increase is the smallest adjustment management need make in any of the factors it controls. All retailers will raise their prices an average of 4 percent. It's the proper response to the political insult. Consumers pay all corporate taxes, hidden or exposed. The retailer will collect the same tax burden he has been collecting all along and pass it on to the government. The state is still collecting 8 percent in taxes on sales, consumers are still paying the 8 percent in taxes on sales, and the 4 percent sales tax receipt is bogus.

But the socialist moron will be so happy. He believes he is paying only half the sales tax burden. The evil corporation is being stiffed for the other half. He is overjoyed. And the politicians will later resume raising sales taxes and claim that the retailers are sharing the consumer's burden.

Would customers be fooled by this ploy? Some might. Would company management be fooled? No. Why then should wage earners believe that their employers match their social security tax contribution?

We shall visit the Social Security tax fraud next. Matching contributions are just another great political lie about who bears the taxes, dear reader. It is just another of many great lies engineered by the United States Congress to maximize your tax load behind your back.

Chapter 46

The Social Security Slush Fund

Imagine a baseball stadium filled with fans. Vendors moving up and down the aisles sell their wares. From a distance it appears that fans in the aisle seats receive the goods and pay the vendors. That a product passes hand to hand one way along the row to a customer in a remote seat and that a payment passes in a like manner in the opposite direction may not be apparent.

In the corporate world it appears that corporations match your social security contribution. But they are playing the role of fans occupying aisle seats. Corporations appear to pay. But they merely pass tax burdens from government in one direction and tax revenue from consumers in the other.

American corporations collect taxes from consumers for the government as required by law. Corporations are legal constructions. They are not taxpayers. Corporate workers can pay taxes, corporate customers can pay taxes, but corporations cannot. But they can be put out of business if they fail to pass the taxes on. Those that survive tax increases pass them on.

Corporate income arrives through sales. A portion of sales income is diverted to the gross cost of labor. But employees do not receive gross pay, they receive net pay. The government seizes a significant part of gross pay for Social Security (SS) and Medicare. Observe the wage pipeline in its simplest form.

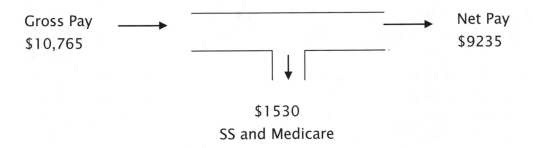

$1530
SS and Medicare

For every 10,765 dollars paid in wages, the worker will receive 9235 dollars. The government will seize 1530 dollars (14.21 percent of gross pay) for Social Security and Medicare.

Comes now the political smoke and mirrors. Observe the wage pipeline after its reconfiguration by government plumbers. Both sets of plumbing have identical inputs and outputs. From a systems engineering viewpoint they are equivalent. But politically the new plumbing serves a new purpose. That purpose is deception.

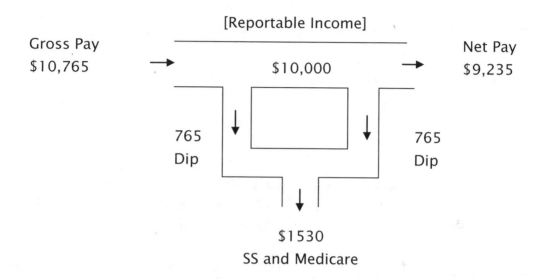

The politicians have defined Social Security income as income existing halfway between the employer's hand and the employee's hand. Note that the total tax is still 1530 dollars, but it now represents 15.3 percent of 10,000 dollars in <u>reportable</u> income. Reportable income is the new political gimmick.

The government is now prepared to double dip. By double dipping in the wage pipeline from the employer's hand to the employee's hand, the government claims that the first dip is from the employer's hand and that the second dip is from the employee's hand.

Sure! And the author is the Easter bunny.

The only thing obvious is that 1530 dollars out of every 10,000 in reported income is seized by government.

Reportable income has merely been defined by law midway between gross labor cost and net income delivered, creating an illusion of two payers for Social Security and Medicare. The worker is urged to believe that his employer matches his social security contribution. Using reportable income as the basis for the income tax adds to the illusion of matching contributions from different payers.

But the employer's alleged contribution is actually a 100 percent income tax bracket on employee income. Social Security taxes arrive with hiring and depart with firing.

New tax burdens will reduce the number of businesses in the landscape and raise the prices of businesses that remain. Those that survive pass tax and labor costs to consumers. Those that failed did not. Taxes lower abundance and raise prices. The higher prices will allow businesses that survive to collect them for government.

Employers offer reportable wages to job seekers. They know that reportable income is an accounting gimmick. The business pays a gross wage and the employee receives a net wage. The government seizes the difference.

It would not affect the employer's bottom line one whit if the employer could pass the gross wage directly to the employee. And if the government then demanded 14.21 percent of employee gross pay for Social Security and Medicare, the change would not affect the employee's bottom line one whit either. However, the employee would know his <u>real</u> Social Security contribution.

Politicians abhor such a grim thought.

All labor carries the same social security burden. That burden (14.21 percent of gross) becomes a fixed part of labor costs. But gross income is a variable that is set by the labor market. And net income is merely the lower amount fixed by law.

If companies cannot find buyers for surwage and tax bloated products, the company's share of the market falls. Labor unions and taxes on labor have decimated many American industries and occupations since passage of the Clayton Act in 1914, the graduated income tax in 1916, and the social security act in 1935. Many blue collar jobs have moved to Southeast Asia.

The author's wife is self employed in the landscape business. She often employs others. She weighs the gross cost of labor when hiring others, but she offers only reportable wages. She knows the game. The labor market continues to set gross wages, and the social security tax continues to set net incomes.

The self employed collect the tax burden from sales as does Corporate America. And they pay slightly less (14.13 percent) of their gross income to government. The tortured calculation is the product of 15.3 times 0.9235 (from IRS pub. 533). Income above one hundred some thousand is not taxed for retirement, but it is taxed for Medicare.

But many workers get that warm fuzzy feeling that they are scalping their employer for half of their retirement. Political lies work. Can you hear the politicians snickering on the Potomac?

Irregardless of how Social Security is funded, the worker may feel that he has a vested interest in the Trust Fund. And the fund is in good hands.

Sorry!

The Supreme Court has ordained that contributors have no property rights in their accounts.[27] By stacking precedent upon precedent the court reached the political decision that the congressional embezzlers wanted. How amazing is that?

No private trust fund could lawfully be plundered in this manner. But the Congress is the trustee. In no body of people anywhere could trust be more misplaced. They have made the trust fund a slush fund. The Congress seizes deposits for earmark spending and the enhancement of congressional careers. The fund is gone, gone, gone. It is part of the national debt.

The Congress will spend any income within its grasp until we have a constitutionally imposed limit on federal spending in dollars per annum.

The dark side of attempts to contain government by constitutional means is that corrupt men interpret constitutional meaning as they see fit. Their oath to uphold the Constitution means nothing to them. By stacking precedent upon precedent a corrupt justice may arrive at any decision imaginable. Constitutional construction should rise from a reading of the Constitution itself and not from a stacking of left leaning precedents.

---

[27] Flemming v. Nestor, 363 U.S. 603 (1960), etal.

On every question of construction, let us carry ourselves back to the time when the constitution was adopted, recollect the spirit manifested in the debates, and instead of trying what meaning may be squeezed out of the text, or invented against it, conform to the probable one in which it was passed.

--Thomas Jefferson—

Chapter 47

The Nature of a Sales Tax

Taxes say a lot about human nature. And it is not very flattering. What they say is that numerous clones of Simon Legree reside in the political landscape and that servitude is far from dead. It is just more covert than overt.

We already know that marginal taxes on income may be shifted from earners to consumers where they reduce a supply of talent in market demand. The tax destroys jobs. The natural mix of labor will regress. It promotes criminal income. Taxes on income do all of these egregious things because they penalize honesty and self improvement. But the distribution of taxes by supply and demand is hidden from the consumer. How many consumers would support the progressive income tax if they knew that consumers pay two thirds of personal income taxes, independent of their own earnings, when they purchase goods or services in inelastic economic demand?

The tax is regressive. Taxes that attempt to harness the productive to favor the indolent, run counter to natural aggregate forces of supply and demand. They result in huge unintended economic consequences. But deception is the name of the taxing game.

Natural market forces will also prevail in distributing the sin taxes on tobacco, alcohol, and gasoline. An increase in the tax on these products will reduce demand by very little. The demand for alcohol, tobacco, and gasoline is inelastic. The buyer pays. The seller collects. The government takes.

Politicians prefer to hide the tax load. Because a sales tax is broad based, it does not target inelastic demand and selected sinners for bleeding as will exorbitant sin taxes. Because it is based on sales, it does not target professional labor for bleeding. It cannot shift career choices and the natural mix of labor. But the sales tax has yet another endearing quality. It can tax income however gained. It does not exclude covert, filched, or welfare acquired income. Thus, the free loading political left abhors the sales tax. They feel your pain.

What are the properties of a fair and just tax as opposed to the existing taxing system that stealthily confiscates all that it can and seeks to avoid retribution by disarming its taxpayers and leaving them subsistence?

- It must be a tax that does not aid or encourage tax evasion by remaining low and impersonal.

- It is a tax that does not require a police state to enforce because it remains low and impersonal.

- It is a tax the state requires only for the legitimate functions of government allowing it to remain low.

- It is a tax that everyone pays thereby minimizing its rate.

- It is a tax that everyone pays, tax payers are the tax beneficiaries, and class warfare is not practiced.

- It is a tax that everyone pays and the electorate is unsoiled by freeloaders who don't share the load.

- It is a tax that is highly visible. It is not buried in the price of consumer products or services like marginal income taxes and corporate taxes.

- It is a tax that is supply and demand neutral. It will not initiate a regression in the natural mix of labor that society, acting through consumer demand, would normally create.

- It is a tax that will not require 1,101 different tax forms and instructions. It will not require 16,339 pages of rules and regulations.[28] It will not require 100,535 enforcers to seize taxes out of selected targets.[29] And it will not require hundreds of thousands of tax consultants to interpret who is targeted and the amount to be seized.[30]

The retail sales tax has all the attributes of fairness. No one is exempt. Paying curbs the appetite of the political left for more government. The widest tax base promotes the smallest tax rate. The states can collect sales taxes for the feds. The IRS can threaten the states instead of threatening politically targeted businesses or individuals with tax audits.

The retail sales tax has an additional attribute that taxes on income do not. If levied on all goods both domestic and imported, it gives no great advantage to imports (as does taxes on American labor) and it simplifies tax implementation.

There is gross harm inflicted on society by **any** taxes on income. They assault honesty and self improvement and they reward criminal income and welfare. They raise the cost of care for the aged and the inept.

A uniform retail sales tax does not futilely attempt a progressive assault on the earned income of free men. A retail sales tax is proportional to personal income but it has no impact on the natural mix of labor. The massive invasion of privacy that personal taxes require is avoided. A retailer will collect the tax from the buyer when he spends. The government need not know the name of the taxpayer. Period!

But there are some who believe that incomes greater than theirs should be seized for their benefit. They wish to avoid taxes. But the only way to avoid income taxes is to avoid honest labor. Wonderful!

Honest labor should not be taxed at all. Honest labor builds affluence. Those who would enslave the productive by law will eventually impoverish and enslave themselves.

---

[28] "Study Uncovers 'Taxing Trend': Complexity Creeping Upward," Capital Ideas, vol. 11, no. 3, pg. 1, May/Jun 2003, National Taxpayers Union Foundation.

[29] Approximate number of IRS employees and Congressmen engaged in tax debauchery.

[30] Author's estimate.

Economist Alan Reynolds has shown that irregardless of how high the marginal income tax rate goes in the United States, revenues will not amount to more than 9 to 11 percent of personal income.[31]

Economically, taxes act no differently than litigation, regulation, or surwages. They are all burdens passed to the market in higher costs. Sales fall and businesses fail. Prices rise as the market shrinks. The buying power of tax revenue falls as consumer spending is removed from private sector production. That is why real tax revenue fails to linearly follow tax increases. It cannot!

But why not minimize our taxes and our economic regression. Why not use taxes only for constraining theft instead of abetting it?

A ten percent uniform retail sales tax on corporate products could readily fund all levels of government in a fully employed society. The author assumes the kind of government the Constitution framed and not the bloated, special interest, damage control budget that taxpayers bear today.

A constitutionally mandated sales tax on retail purchases for raising federal revenue would give the government incentive to free private enterprise by visibly tying government buying power to private sector productivity.

Let the government view a robust economy as a taxing asset rather than see taxpayers as a lawn to be mowed at subsistence level. Let the government see the stock market as an indicator of economic health rather than competition to the national debt for investment money. The national debt, the stock market, and the Federal Reserve will be linked in Part VII. The reader will not be pleased.

Government is a form of insurance that you buy for the protection of your property and for the protection of your rights. If you accumulate more wealth, you have more to lose. You should pay more for insuring it. The sales tax installs a linear relationship between income and government provided insurance.

---

[31] Cited from Eileen Ciesla, "Laetitia's Lament", The American Spectator, June 01, pg. 49.

There should be no tax exemptions unless they are impersonal. Personal exemptions require a gross invasion of privacy and a huge bureaucracy. The very concept of a personal tax is inimical to personal liberty.

Willie Sutton robbed banks because of their ability to pay. Attempts to tax on an ability to pay are theft. One knows that if he possesses the integrity of the civilized man.

> **See if the law benefits one citizen at the expense of another by doing what the citizen himself cannot do without committing a crime. Then abolish that law without delay.**
>
> —Frederic Bastiat—

Chapter 48

The Betrayal of Trust

When one realizes that the marginal taxes on honestly earned high income are largely shifted to consumers by supply and demand and he realizes that taxes on lower income are shifted hardly at all, one wonders why the Congress cannot trash this monstrous and ugly dysfunctional tax and replace it with a simple non invasive sales tax. At least a sales tax is proportional to income.

But the income tax is stealthy. It maximizes revenue. And politicians love it.

The leftist news media may admit to an average tax load approaching half of all earnings. But the average means nothing. As someone once said, the average person has one tit and one testicle.

There is no average taxpayer. There are taxpayers and there are tax beneficiaries. If one receives benefits that he will not pay for, he is a tax beneficiary. And if one pays for benefits that he will not receive, he is a typical taxpayer. The Congress has divided the people and set them one upon another.

The Constitutional duty of the House of Representatives is to represent taxpayers and only taxpayers. The House has betrayed that trust.

> **Article. I. Section. 2. ...Representatives and direct Taxes shall be apportioned among the several States which may be included within this Union, according to their respective Numbers, which shall be determined by adding to the whole Number of free Persons, including those bound to Service for a Term of Years, and excluding Indians not taxed, three fifths of all other Persons**...

The incongruous 'three fifths' arose over a method to apportion seats to slave states. Are slaves to be counted as taxpayers? Should slave states be rewarded with more seats? Note also that Indians not taxed are not to be counted in the apportionment. The opening statement reads, Representatives and direct taxes shall be apportioned... The intent of the founders is obvious. Taxes and House seats are to be bundled together. Those not taxed are not to be counted in the apportionment of seats. The House was to represent the taxpayers.

> **Article. I. Section. 7. All bills for raising revenue shall originate in the House of Representatives**...

Again we see that the House was to represent the interests of the taxpayer. Bills for raising revenue may arise nowhere else.

Granting to organized labor the political power to seize surwages from corporations is essentially granting the political power to tax to a private collective and is unconstitutional on its face. Nothing in the Constitution suggests that federal power to seize money can be ceded to the private sector.

The fourteenth amendment to the Constitution removed the words <u>and direct taxes</u> from section 2. The unbundling of taxes from the apportionment of House seats was initiated as far back as 1868.

The betrayal of the taxpayer adds a significant load to the taxpayer's burden. Every taxpayer carries someone else on his back.

> **The state is the great fiction by which everybody seeks to live at the expense of everybody else.**

> —Frederic Bastiat—

Chapter 49

Damage Control in Perpetuity

The tyrannical federal tax burden on the taxpayer is the partial result of the fact that millions of tax beneficiaries do not contribute. But there is another part to the federal tax burden. It is the cost of alleviating continuous economic losses. It is damage control.

Unemployment arises when government symbionts coerce wages above market. More taxes are then needed to provide unemployment benefits. Unemployment benefits can be eliminated by ending the surwages. The salient character of free enterprise is full employment.

Wage gaps also arise from the coercion of wages. There could be ten laborers earning below average wages so that one may earn the wages of many far above the average. The proper way to raise the minimum wage is to stop the coercion of surwages. The wage gaps will narrow and return to an earned distribution, the finest distribution possible.

Low wages and labor surpluses expand the ranks of welfare. The buying power of minimum wages would be much greater if surwages, taxes on income, and unemployment burdens were to end. Gross pay could be take home pay. The dollar would buy far more. The future could be so very bright.

Instead, taxes are out of control. Minimum wages are at subsistence level. Criminal income is attractive and tax free. The drug culture attracts more recruits. The future offers only more taxes, more crime, and more poverty.

This is your government at work.

More than half of personal income tax revenue collected by Washington is required to pay interest on the national debt. We can slash our federal taxes by a default of the federal debt and return the principle in appreciated dollars. The stimulus to the economy could be fabulous and permanent.

The ramifications of federal debt and a means of retiring it are the subject of Part VII.

Social security accounts must belong to the contributor and the entitlement made proportional to contributions. Government can act as an insurer instead of an embezzler.

The public costs of the legal system could be reduced. It could be converted to a loser pays system as widely practiced in Europe since Roman times. Class action lawsuits and unlimited damage awards contribute to rising medical costs, to rising insurance costs, to rising energy costs, and to rising taxes. The legal profession has created a source of welfare for millionaires.

When welfare (for the elite and for the indolent), surwages, and public debt are removed from the federal landscape and the value of the dollar greatly increased by real productivity, a single digit federal tax on corporate retail sales should be quite sufficient for funding the legitimate role of the federal government.

Free enterprise does not engage in economic destruction nor does it create a need for welfare. And free enterprise never cheapens the dollar. The United States Congress does all these things and more.

But nothing will be done until the **political problem** is corrected. The political problem is that the Congress will do anything at any cost to elicit campaign funds and remain in office.

Part vii
The National Debt

The national debt is a huge taxpayer drain today and it represents a worsening disaster of immense dimensions. The debt has been distributed globally in the form of interest paying bills, notes, and bonds. Both private investors and foreign governments have purchased them.

Public debt instruments compete with the private stock market for investment money. When the stock market is bullish, investors tend to cash in debt instruments at maturity and invest their funds in the stock market.

But the government is broke. It cannot pay its debt or pay higher interest rates on it. When the government is threatened with higher returns from the stock market it will initiate monetary policies to bring the economy and the stock market down.

The political collusion is between the Congress and the Federal Reserve Banking System. Most people have no clue that more than half of their income tax is used to pay interest on national debt. That money goes to investors both foreign and domestic. Nor do they know that the seven trillion dollar loss in the stock market and in their retirement plans in the year 2000 was deliberately brought upon them. Incredibly, they still seek out the perpetrators of their economic woes for a solution.

Chapter 50

The National Debt

Government should never be allowed to borrow money. The private individual knows that he will have to return the money he borrows. He will either pay or it will be confiscated from his estate. And if the individual has no fiscal integrity he can find no credit and assume no debt. Government has no fiscal integrity either, but then it doesn't need it. Government holds the gun.

The national debt is a product of political embezzlement and fraud. It is embezzlement because much of the money was taken from trust funds. It was improperly used. It is fraud because whether borrowed from trust funds or from the marketing of interest bearing bills, notes, and bonds, the Congress does not intend to pay the principle back.

Those who hold debt instruments profit from taxpayer paid interest. Debt holders see national debt as an asset, not a liability. And the Federal Reserve System holds a considerable portion of the national debt as interest bearing assets. The taxpayer will pay interest on the debt in perpetuity.

The national debt should not be thought of as the number of centuries it will take to pay it back and therefore of little interest to matters of the day. It should be thought of as the amount of personal income tax you pay today (roughly half and rising) simply to pay interest to debt holders.

Politicians had embezzled 10 trillion dollars by the close of 2008 by forging the taxpayer's name onto debt instruments. They did so to purchase the tax beneficiary vote and to fund damage control. They stay in the ruling class. The taxpayer stays in the indebted class.

And consider whom the Congress blames for the national debt. The taxpayers! The taxpayers have not matched Congressional appetites. The tax payers will not spend their money right.

Lyndon Baines Johnson initiated budget wangling during his administration. LBJ wanted to hide the cost of the Viet Nam war from the American public by offsetting those costs against Social Security surpluses. During the Nixon presidency, the Congress in a hissy fit passed an act requiring the president to spend all appropriations. So there is a spending frenzy by federal managers as each fiscal year comes to a close. Jimmy Carter later took the country off the annual zero based budget system and indexed all programs to inflation. This single factor contributed greatly to the explosion in spending under Reagan. The political left continues to blame the early Reagan tax cuts for the deficit. But the cuts boosted economic activity. And the Internal Revenue Service doubled gross annual tax collections over the Reagan decade.

From 1983 to 1986, President Reagan and the Congress raised Social Security and Medicare taxes and reformed military and civil service retirement to ostensibly build surpluses for paying future benefits. The six trust funds are military retirement, civil service retirement, supplementary medical insurance, Medicare hospital insurance, disability insurance, and old age & survivors insurance (social security). The six funds have accumulated more than 2.5 trillion in surpluses. [32]

The reported surpluses, however, are bogus. The surplus is in treasury IOUs. It is only more paper promising to pay. And you know what a politician's promise is worth.

But the money has been spent. It is gone, gone, gone.

Bill Clinton claimed budget surpluses while in office. But like Lynden Johnson he used social security and 'creative' accounting. The liberal press promoted the lie. The last real budget surplus occurred under Dwight Eisenhower in 1957.[33]

Many in the Congress want the people to view tax cuts with alarm. Tax cuts are blamed for any increase in national debt. But the Congress will spend any money in its grasp. What the government cannot borrow it will counterfeit by simply raising the debt limit. And many leftist members of the Congress want the taxpayers disarmed. They know what they have done and they intend to continue doing it.

---

[32] Website of Gene Taylor, Representative, 4th district, Mississippi, 15 Jan 04.

[33] Laurence M. Vance, "Lessons from a Bloated Budget", Freedom Daily, Nov 2010, Pg. 29

One cannot make minimum payments on his credit card debt with his credit card. One would never have to repay the debt nor pay the interest. But the Congress pays interest on borrowed funds with IOUs. It bears repeating. The Congress has no intention to retire federal debt. The taxpayers can bear the interest load forever.

Today's problem is the interest paid on that portion of the national debt that has been marketed. Private investors will not accept IOU's in payment of interest. IOUs will buy nothing. Interest payments on the marketed debt must be made in cash on demand.

The marketed federal debt is roughly 5 trillion dollars (2008). It is dispersed in interest bearing bills, notes, and bonds. The Federal Reserve continues to cheapen the value of the dollar forcing the private sector to shun the holding of dollars and to purchase interest paying debt instruments. The retirement funding and the insurance backing of all Americans instead of being invested in the private sector has been borrowed and spent by the United States Congress.

As 2008 closed the total federal debt reached 10 trillion (10,000,000,000,000) dollars. Of that amount, 2.7 trillion is owed to foreign creditors including China and Japan. The interest paid on Congressional debt per annum is over half of individual income tax revenue collected per annum.

What could debt managers do if interest earned in the private stock market were to rise and remain above that returned on maturing federal debt instruments for any amount of time? Investors would cash in debt instruments at maturity and turn to private stock. There would be a run on the treasury.

That will not be allowed. The feds will employ damage control. The Federal Reserve System must periodically bash the economy to prevent the stock market from soaring and threatening government debt instruments with better returns.

A severe bashing began in 2000. The Congress pretended to have no clue. They will whine about the bashing but the dysfunctional Congress will do nothing. The whine is only for public consumption.

We will look at the political efforts to conceal the consequences of runaway debt from the American people next. It's a despicable if not criminal act cloaked from public view by another great federal falsehood, an **overheated economy**.

Chapter 51

The Overheated Economy

The Federal Reserve's first great milestone was initiating and sustaining chronic inflation. Their second great milestone was initiating the great depression (by deflating the money supply). Their third great milestone could be one of initiating and sustaining a depression in perpetuity with immense wage gaps and an accompanying high crime rate. It will arise as the feds periodically fight an alleged war on an **overheated economy.**

Remember, dear reader, that the landscape is full of, ahem, political lies. Well hold your nose and hike up your pants legs because we are about to wade through another deep and magnificent political lie.

> **The growth rate for 1999 has reached 6.9 percent. The Federal Reserve must continue to raise interest rates to constrain consumer spending and prevent the economy from overheating.** [34]

Overheating? The economy must be slowed? This is sheer nonsense. An economy does not overheat. An economy will seek full employment in the absence of political interference. At full employment, a labor shortage will limit further expansion. Overheating is not found in old college economic texts. It's a new political alibi. But what is its purpose?

> **The feds want to slow our economy and limit economic growth to around 3 percent per year. Any greater growth could trigger inflation.** [35]

------

[34] Jeannine Aversa, " Blazing Economy Grows Hotter," Associated Press, Cited in The Sun, 26 Feb 00.
[35] Ibid.

Aha! We are to believe that unchecked economic growth triggers inflation. But that is not true. It is just another of many great political lies.

The first law of economics in a nutshell is expressed in the inverse algebraic relation between the average price levels and production.

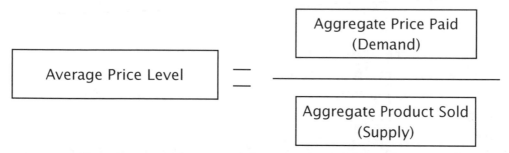

Market supply is proportional to man hours of production. Market demand is proportional to man hours of earning. So velocity will affect demand and supply pretty much the same. So the average price level will not change with economic velocity. Price levels depend on the money supply.

The second law of economics in a nutshell is expressed in the inverse algebraic relation between wage rates and employment.

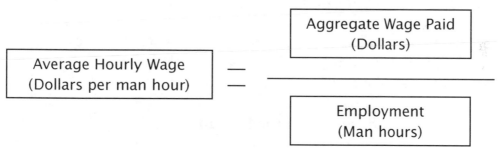

Velocity is proportional to man hours of productivity. The aggregate wage paid and employment in man hours will rise or fall with velocity. The numerator and the denominator of the fraction are affected equally. So their ratio, the average hourly wage, remains independent of velocity. Velocity will increase until full employment is reached. At full employment velocity can increase no further. Full employment is a natural limit on velocity. And it is an optimum condition.

The Federal Reserve raised interest rates by a quarter percent Tuesday, saying that strong growth and low unemployment had left the economy vulnerable to inflation. The feds

emphasized a concern that the economy is running out of workers and that pressure to raise wages and prices will mount.[36]

There is no end to federal lies. Velocity by itself cannot affect prices. And while velocity does affect the aggregate wage, it does not affect the average wage.

So where is the fabled pressure to raise wages and prices? The average wage level cannot climb unless the money supply increases. And the average price level cannot climb unless the money supply increases or production per man hour falls. So leave the damn money supply alone!

There is no threat of inflation from the people. The threat is from the government. The feds are merely creating a colossal alibi for slowing economic velocity. And why would they want to do that?

A reduction in velocity (the number of times the money supply will pass from buyers to sellers per annum) cannot reduce inflation because both demand (aggregate price paid) and supply (aggregate product sold) will fall with the reduction in flow. But when velocity falls, so must employment. How can the feds justify throwing huge numbers of people out of work?

My latest and most politically correct economics book defines an <u>overheated economy</u> as one in which the actual rate of unemployment is less than the natural rate of unemployment.

Oh my gawd! We could suffer **overemployment**!

But a natural rate of unemployment is merely a government created decoy. The feds have admitted their goal. It is to limit our economic growth. Three percent is the goal of the day. Thanks to the deficit spending of a career seeking Congress, prosperity is a threat instead of a dream.

The government must engineer an excuse for slowing the economy. Some economists may have been fooled. Others could be sources of economic misinformation in the media.

---

[36] Richard W. Stevenson, "Latest increase aimed at preventing inflation," N.Y.Times News Service, Cited in Bremerton Sun, 17 Nov 1999.

Here is the overheat theory in a nut shell. In an overheated economy factories are run around the clock. Many workers work overtime. Labor costs climb. Costs will spread to the market. Therefore inflation is triggered.

But sustaining overtime wages is only possible if the buyer is willing to pay a premium for early delivery of a product. The payment of premium labor costs for some will take potential wages from others, just as surwages do. Some gain and some lose. Overtime at worst could merely increase the wage gaps.

Overemployment and overheating are both political fictions.

What if the stock market did not suffer unintended damage in the federal attack on the dollar per annum flow, dear reader? What if the <u>stock market was the intended target?</u>

How could the Federal Reserve justify a deliberate bashing of the private economy, throwing millions of people out of work, and screwing half of American households out of seven trillion dollars in the stock market?

Saving the national debt from a default would be a top priority of the feds and other debt investors. No one needs to know their political perfidy.

Government faces competition from the stock market for investment money. The government does not have the trillions necessary to cash out debt instruments in investor portfolios at maturity nor the additional hundreds of billions necessary to pay greater competitive interest. The stock market must take a fall.

Beginning in late 1999 and continuing through 2000 the Federal Reserve bashed and they bashed the economy with one interest rate hike after another until the stock market fell.

The rise in interest rates raised the cost of credit. People borrowed less. People spent less. Corporations then produced less. They shed excess labor. Employment fell. And the stock market fell.

Investors must be frightened away from the purchase of 'risky' private stock and coaxed into the renewal of 'safe' government issued bills, notes, and bonds as they reach maturity.

The Congress could slash federal spending to free up revenue for paying greater competitive interest on the debt. But the Congress would not do that. Careers in the Congress depend on the feed and care of tax beneficiaries. The feds know that. The feds only option is to elude a default by limiting economic growth and slamming the stock market. The Congress has them squeezed between a rock and a hard place.

The alleged limit on economic growth has **nothing** to do with the bogus political invention conned on us as an overheated economy. It has **every thing** to do with containing the costs of interest on the national debt.

Workers must be sacrificed to keep the lid on growth and limit stock market performance. Unemployment shall periodically soar because of the national debt and federal manipulation of bank loan rates.

Note the political convenience of finding the actual rate of unemployment to be less than a natural rate of unemployment. Too many are employed. The natural rate can be restored by throwing millions out of work. Nice!

Corrupt labor laws and funny money have created economic links between the money supply, the aggregate wage, and employment. The feds can shrink the money supply, shrink the wage supply, shrink the labor force, and shrink production. Consequently the feds can lower the performance of the stock market until government debt instruments again attract investment money.

The national debt avoids a default, the butts of the trust fund raiders in the United States Congress are covered, and federal bankers and other debt investors continue to suck up more than half of individual income tax revenue in interest payments on marketed federal debt. Neat!

The Congress will not cut spending to pay down the national debt, and they will not raise taxes to pay down the debt either. That lie has been advanced for numerous tax increases over several decades.

Actually, the debt cannot be paid down with tax increases. It is far too large. A prosperous economy is required to carry the tax load. But a politically restrained economy is required to suppress the stock market and retain public investment in the national debt. The feds are plodding down a narrow political path between economic lethargy and bankruptcy. The debt is out of control.

The feds reduced the nation's currency and deflated the stock market initiating the Great Depression. Then the feds lost control to the socialist morons in the Congress. What will the Congress do in the new century? We can not expect the toads to become princes.

The Federal Reserve's assault on the stock market resulted in an estimated seven trillion dollar loss. The marketed federal debt was roughly four trillion at the time. Why did the government slam stock holders instead of debt holders?

The feds want to deflect blow back away from felonious government onto innocent private enterprise. Damage control is their game. Is it any wonder that socialist morons fault private enterprise for economic disasters?

For nearly a century, government has cheapened the dollar for political benefit. But an <u>appreciating dollar</u> is the way out. It is the only way out. Monies invested in debt will appreciate if the dollar appreciates. Debt holders will not suffer a loss when interest payments are defaulted.

An appreciating dollar is <u>economically</u> possible with a Constitutional limit on federal spending in dollars. But it may be politically impossible.

O what tangled webs we weave, when first we practice to deceive.

A balanced budget amendment will not do. Tax increases will not do. They depreciate the buying power of the dollar. The dollar must be appreciated. And payment of interest on the debt must be defaulted.

Once payment of interest on federal debt is eliminated, the stock market cannot be seen as a competitive threat to government issued debt. It will remove the Federal Reserve's motive for clamping a speed limit on our economic growth.

Once the political power to seize money from corporate America is removed from the insatiable greed of organized labor, the expansion of the money supply to offset unemployment can stop.

Once the expansion of the money supply ceases our trade will balance.

But expanding the money supply will not cease until a Constitutional limit on total federal expenditures limits Congressional spending. That limit must be fixed in dollars. And it must cut as well as limit government spending or the dollar will not appreciate.

Retirement funds could be invested in the stock market and the market immunized from its only real threats, the Federal Reserve System and the United States Congress. The stock market represents a real <u>investment in America</u>. Federal debt represents only an <u>investment in political larceny</u>.

> **I...place economy among the first and most important of republican virtues, and public debt as the greatest of the dangers to be feared**...
>
> **--Thomas Jefferson--**
>
> In a letter to William Plummer,
> 1816.

Chapter 52

A Murder Scene

One hears a gunshot in another room. He runs in to investigate. Mr. Fed is holding the smoking gun. Mr. Debt is cowering behind him. Mr. Market is lying belly up on the floor.

Mr. Fed says he had to do it. Mr. Market was out of control.

But Mr. Debt owes Mr. Market vast sums of money. Money he does not have. And he will not now have to pay. Criminal investigators would call this motive. This is obviously a crime scene. Do you think Mr. Debt and Mr. Fed who have a profitable partnership with Market money are innocent?

Here are some Greenspan comments taken from his sworn testimony to Congress.

> **The failure of economic models...contributed to the recent persistent under prediction of economic growth and over prediction of inflation...**
>
> **While this stellar, non inflationary economic expansion still appears remarkably stress free on the surface, there are developing imbalances that give us pause...**
>
> **Nonetheless, the persistence of certain imbalances poses a risk to the long run outlook.**
>
> **Bubbles generally are perceptible only after the fact. To spot a bubble in advance requires a judgment that hundreds of thousands of informed investors have it all wrong.**[37]

Economic sense can often be communicated clearly with only a minimum of words necessary to add depth to the premise, but nonsense is characterized by an excess of words never quite arriving at coherency.

What did we hear from the former chairman?

Chapter 53

In the Aftermath

It is a decrease in the money flow through corporate America that constitutes a business slowdown. Changes in government monetary or fiscal policy and changes in consumer borrowing and spending determine if the aggregate flow of cash shall increase or decrease.

---

[37] www.federalreserve.gov/boarddocs/testimony/1999

The Federal Reserve triggered the last recession when they began their repeated bashing of the economy in late 1999 by repeatedly raising interest rates. They reduced the money flow through corporate America by tightening credit. Consumers borrowed less. Banks borrowed less. The reserve multiplier kicked in. The money supply declined. Corporate income declined. The number of jobs in the private sector declined.

But in January 2001 the Federal Reserve began backpedaling like crazy. Their actions had pulled down stock market performance **as planned**, but it had also reduced federal revenue and expanded deficit spending in the Congress (the Bush White House will receive the blame).

By June of 2003 the feds had lowered the discount rate (thirteen times) to its lowest point in one half century to stimulate an increase in consumer spending. The fed had obviously lost control. Raising the discount rate strongly curtails consumer spending. But in the recession that results, lowering the discount rate does almost nothing. The public will not borrow when their jobs are threatened. The feds can pull a string but they cannot push it.

If the stock market recovers and threatens the national debt with better investment returns in the future, the feds must repeat their business bashing.

As 2008 drew to a close a long market surge in real estate sales ended in an unprecedented number of mortgage defaults and bankruptcies. The 2008 disaster is the unintended consequence of Congressional attempts at social engineering by pushing the private banking sector into high risk loans. The game was initiated in Carter times with the Community Reinvestment Act and pushed by political threat to the banking industry during the reign of Clinton.

The feds bashing of the stock market in 2000 drove many investors out of the stock market and into real estate. That inflated a real estate market that was already over leveraged from high risk loans. Bush II will be blamed for the economic disaster because the ugly weed of Congressional corruption blossomed during his reign.

A decade later (July 2010) the leftists in the Congress, who continuously engineer economic disasters and always attribute to others the blame, spewed forth yet another damage control bill. The Dodd-Frank Financial Reform Act was enacted to correct an alleged felonious financial market. This bill is the act of a desperate Congress attempting to frame the private sector for its own misfeasance when the Congress forced the home finance market to engage in high risk loans.

Interestingly enough, the Congress called upon the principle perpetrators of the economic disaster in the House and Senate to lend their names to the damage control bill. Do not expect any indictments!

The growth of national debt accelerates as government bailouts proliferate. The debt will be defaulted. The hammer will fall. The damage control game must eventually run its course.

The growth of national debt began with the 'great society'. The dysfunctional Congress is the guilty party. The Congress controls the federal purse. The feds are surely contemplating other means of damage control. But will the Congress go along? There is a communication problem. And the Congress in the aggregate is an economic zero.

Those who are aware of the political betrayal of public trust must conceal their knowledge of it. The Congress and the feds cannot communicate. And those in the economic dark can only worsen a bad situation.

When the next bashing comes, the mother of all depressions may fall out of it. However, the last bashing may have already initiated the destruction sequence.

Or the Congress could appreciate the dollar by drastically <u>cutting</u> and constitutionally <u>limiting</u> federal spending to an explicit sum of dollars per annum, freeze the money supply and create the economic equivalent of a gold standard, zero the interest payments on debt, rescind labor laws, rescind all taxes on income, phase in an honest sales tax in lieu of hidden taxes on retail sales, and stand aside.

Private enterprise would leap forward. Employers will set wages for full employment. Wage gaps will narrow to an optimum spread. Velocity will find a natural level determined by the number of hours we as individuals in the aggregate wish to work per annum, unfettered by public perception of economic doom, and perturbed only by natural disturbances and the Holiday Season. The political sores of inflation, stagflation, widening wage gaps, recessions, or depression will not be possible. Our standard of living will soar.

Part viii

Politics

The proof of betrayal of trust by the federal government is in the preponderance of the evidence. The reader knows at this point that the government has totally corrupted the field of economics with political lies and egregious legislation. Unfortunately there is much more.

The United States faces an energy shortage of dire consequences. She has become dependent on foreign oil. Environmentalists have trashed the finest alternative possible by demonizing nuclear power. We have also become dependent on foreign made steel, foreign made machines and subassemblies, and foreign made consumer products. Consequently the balance of trade widens. The political power of organized labor and of environmental zealots far exceeds their proportion in the political landscape and their economic destruction of America is immense and growing.

We have replaced intelligent decisions in the private sector with insane decisions in the political sector. A small part of the damage the symbionts have wrought with legislation bought and sold will be presented.

Chapter 54

The Sins of Democracy

The founders did not give us a democracy. The founders gave us a republic. The republic was to represent taxpayers. But it no longer does so. It represents special interests.

Democracy is two wolves and a lamb deciding on whom to have for dinner. If the lamb has no rights it is meat for the majority. A majority is not a license for unmitigated seizure of minority earnings. Not in a civil society. The socialist sees it differently. But socialists have never created a civil society. They have only pulled them down.

Democracy works in a coercion free environment. A local fraternal organization may pass motions by majority vote. But it is careful to weigh the opinion of the minority who can quit the organization and withdraw dues support.

The American taxpayer cannot quit the federal government. The IRS will seek him out for an additional ten years of tax servitude wherever on earth he flees. No other countries are so venomous.

Juries do not convict on a mere majority either. It takes a unanimous jury to convict on a capital offense and a super majority on lesser convictions.

A majority of one at the ballot box could be the difference between exercising birth control and committing murder in government eyes. That is absurd. Super majorities are necessary to justify super punishment. And no politically wise jury should convict where a draconian punishment follows a minor legal infringement. Juries must represent the people, not the state. Juries can refuse to convict just as prosecutors can refuse to prosecute.

The rights of the minority have no protection in a democracy. One must rely on a unanimous jury to protect himself from the majority of one in a court room. But where among taxpayers does one find the rights of the minority protected?

Majorities are fine for electing people, but they are not justification for taking ones rights or property. Not if we are to be a free people.

Parliaments cannot pass every act on a majority of one either. Parliamentary rules normally require a two thirds majority to end debate and move to a vote on the question. One third of the membership plus one can block onerous legislation from passage by engaging in a filibuster. A simply majority can end the debate, but only by a motion to table the issue.

The rules of debate have two purposes. They are to promote the will of the majority, and to protect the rights of the minority.

A minority can never pass legislation, but a significant minority may block issues of extreme repugnance to them with a filibuster. Parliaments are not democracies, dear reader. **The minority has rights**.

In 1975 the political left in the U.S. Senate changed the rules of debate. Under an alibi of fairness, which they always deploy, they reduced the protection of the minority. A smaller majority (60 in lieu of 67) can now screw the minority. The leftist media which usually touts the rights of minorities cloaked this event with silence. Note the two faces of the left.

In November of 2008 state voters removed a sixty percent rule and a quorum requirement for passage of new property taxes in Washington. The leftoids in the Seattle ringworm overwhelmed property owners across the state positioning them for revenue rape. Their alibi was fairness.

The political tragedy is that many voters in the nanny state are not taxpayers. They are tax beneficiaries. They should not be voting on issues they will not pay for. Period!

Rebellions occur when tax beneficiaries attempt to enslave tax payers. The American tax rebellion in 1776 resulted in a Republic. The Republic was to represent the taxpayers. The English monarchy did not.

Politicians never earn their income through public demand as taxpayers must. Consequently many view taxes as their entitlements. And taxpayers can never pay enough. The appetite of tax beneficiaries is never sated. Greed prevails over need when armed by law.

The Congress has set tax beneficiaries upon tax payers. Class warfare elicits campaign funds for the class warriors in the Congress. But a growing number of taxpayers do not see a significant difference between thugs and politicians except that those in government will deny them much more wealth than the private thug ever could.

The sins of democracy are that it allows class warfare. Class warfare elicits funds for the reelection of incumbents. That much has been shown. Democracy is pulling us toward a tyranny of elitist special interests and economic ruin. We should not be forcing our dysfunctional democracy on the rest of the world. We should be promoting free enterprise and limited government in house. We need to resolve our own problems with democracy and lead the world, if we may, only by example.

Chapter 55

Load Limits

Nations have politically set boundaries. Within the boundary there live enormous numbers of people. But there are limits on capacity. Every container has its limits. Bridges have load limits. Life boats and elevators have capacities. Nations too will have reasonable capacities for harboring populations. If the United States cannot gain control of its borders, she will become a refugee camp for the indolent.

No one wants to live in a refugee camp. Food resources are overwhelmed. Water resources are overwhelmed. Toilet facilities are overwhelmed. Shelter is overwhelmed. Health care is overwhelmed.

Taxpayers do not want to see the United States overrun by illegal immigration. Neither should environmentalists. At some point the nation will be overwhelmed by the tax load, the living environment will deteriorate, and the ingress of foreigners will grind to a halt. Our house will no longer be a nice place to live.

That does not need to happen. Others need only do what America did in 1789. The world can be a much nicer place if all nations adopted limited government and an economic policy of Laissez Faire. We need to return to our roots, rebuild our home, and set it as an example and not a place for freeloaders to crash.

It is amazing how many people oppose closing our frontier. Some people will not face natural limits. Their ideology overrides logic. The flood of illegal labor puts unskilled labor in a buyers market. Employers seek untaxed labor. And the political left seeks their illegal vote. Yeah! Aliens register to vote.

Liberal court decisions have made it impossible to deny public benefits such as schools and medical services to illegal entrants. And illegal entrants need only have a baby within our borders to access entrance to the Unwed Motherhood. But they do not pay income taxes. They pull themselves up by pulling taxpayers down. They are leftist by nature. We are not gaining human assets. We are gaining human liabilities.

There is a way to control our borders. And it won't require building a great fence. Citizens and legal immigrants could be issued national ID. The human genome encoded in DNA could verify family lineage and prove citizenship. We must deny employment and public benefits to illegal entrants and their babies wherever born. They could be visitors but not squatters.

The political left will scream about national ID. Why that would invade the border crasher's right of privacy.

Exactly! Americans have no secrets from the government. The IRS knows where they live, where they lived, where they work, and where they worked. The IRS knows their earnings, their tips, their inheritance, their gifts, their divorces, their child support, their alimony, their dependents, their interest, their savings, their investments, their barters, their winnings, everything. What does the IRS not know about taxpaying Americans?

It is time to reveal the truth. Are tax beneficiaries Americans? Or are American leftists enslaving America to an illegal, left leaning, voting bloc?

The IRS can issue national identification to taxpayers. They have the data. They can merge with the Immigration and Naturalization Service (INS). House seats can be apportioned to the states in accordance with their tax paying population. And that is still a Constitutional imperative.

Legal immigrants must demonstrate their ability for self support. Border crashers meet no such constraints. Will aliens be protected from exposure as tax beneficiaries and as illegally registered voters? Will aliens be allowed anonymity while the privacy of American taxpayers is totally invaded by government?

A few years ago a man in California registered his dog to vote. He did it to unmask the system. The ruse came to light when the dog was called for jury duty. That is how easy it is to register. Anywhere!

Welfare agencies everywhere are blocked from checking the citizenship of their caseloads. The taxpayer is bashed. The 1986 amnesty act doubled the flow of border crashers into the country.

Many serious issues facing our country today cannot be addressed until a national disaster initiates damage control. But damage control goes on and on. The problems need to be fixed and the losses ended. But the Congress cannot fix them. The Congressional puppets dance on the strings of election contributors and they are totally dysfunctional.

The government cannot block terrorist infiltration, it cannot block drug infiltration, and it cannot block welfare infiltration. And when guns are banned the government will not block gun infiltration either.

When our population stops growing by illegal invasion, the feds could freeze the money supply and create an economic gold standard. Constitutional limits on federal spending become palatable. But the seizure of surwages must end to eliminate wage gaps, unemployment, and inflation. Only then can the vicious wage price spiral initiated by organized labor and the feds be ended. Only then will the wage gaps naturally narrow to an economic optimum.

Unfortunately, the dysfunctional Congress can do nothing but dig us into a deeper hole. They will not risk their careers. And they will take America down with them. The strings on the Congressional puppets must be severed.

Chapter 56

Self Defense

In or around September of 1999, CBS devoted an entire Evening News segment to convincing the American people that the Second Amendment was never intended to give individuals a right to keep and bear arms.[38]

On 26 June 2008 the political ideology of the left was abruptly reversed. The Supreme Court found the second amendment to be an individual right and that people could keep guns in the home for self defense.

You are well aware of the leftist plan for apportioning the wealth of others at this milestone in the manuscript. They have seized all that they dare without provoking taxpayer retribution. They want the taxpayer disarmed. The leftist media does also.

The Second Amendment reads,

> **A well regulated militia being necessary to the security of a free state, the right of the people to keep and bear arms shall not be infringed.**

The subject of the amendment is the right of the people to keep and bear arms. This right of the people shall not be infringed. The opening phrase links this right to the security of a free state. People in captivity are disarmed.

The founders recalled the atrocities committed by the British occupation. They listed them in the Declaration of Independence. The founders did not want the new government to replace militias with another potential army of occupation. They wanted armed citizens for the defense of the community and federal infringement of the right of the people to keep and bear arms is expressly forbidden.

---

[38] NRA-ILA letter to members dated 30 September 99.

A militia can be sworn into duty just like a posse. The Second amendment is a restraining order placed against the federal government. The people are not to be disarmed.

That should be enough, but there is more. The Ninth Amendment reads,

> **The enumeration in the Constitution of certain rights shall not be construed to deny or disparage others retained by the people.**

The ninth amendment gives no suggestion that rights enumerated in the Constitution are created by its adoption. Instead it directs that the new government is not to deny or disparage any rights of the people. Period!

The Declaration of Independence further defined human rights,

> **We hold these truths to be self evident, that all men are created equal, that they are endowed by their creator with certain unalienable rights,...that to secure these rights, governments are instituted among men**...

Human rights are endowed by nature or by God, not by government. The purpose of government is to secure human rights. The intentions of the founders are clear. The meaning of the second amendment was never in doubt for much of our history. But leftoids fear an armed electorate.

Leftists and their patsies in the media will have us believe that the right to bear arms belongs only to the militia. But the authority of a soldier to bear arms has never required an expressed right. It is understood. Arms impart authority. An enumerated right of the people to bear arms shares authority with free citizens. Were it not an individual right, there is no purpose in expressing it.

The right expresses the conjunctive keep and bear. Keep designates private ownership. Bear designates a right to carry.

The Supreme Court decision was a narrow five to four victory for individual rights. Liberals on the bench remain eager to curtail human rights. This decision can be reversed by presidential appointees to the court. Obama may make the appointment. Witness the recent liberal infringement of property rights and freedom of speech. People who rule are careless of human rights. <u>They do not need them</u>. But those who are ruled rely on them.

In the summer of 2008, five men sought out and found the original meaning of the right to bear arms. Three men and one woman found what could be invented against its origin. Thomas Jefferson certainly anticipated the perfidy of those holding political power.

Thugs cannot be disarmed. A right to keep and bear arms is a threat only to thugs who would target others for theft. It is a threat to the political left who would steal under the color of law.

The crime rate in Australia and in the United Kingdom has soared since their citizens have been disarmed. The leftist media remains silent on this immensely important consequence of disarming a free people and relegating them to a political pecking order.

We live in an uncivil world. Self defense has always been the responsibility of the individual. You should not have to die because an elite group of professional liars, politicians, had promised to disarm your killer.

Chapter 57

Environmental Fraud

Science, as well as economics, has been corrupted by politics. The Congress in its blind pursuit of the campaign funds or the votes of zealots creates environmental crisis, medical crisis, energy crisis, a banking crisis, or some other unintended consequence. There are common elements in every crisis. Incumbents initially profit by them. Zealots or special interests continue to profit by them. And taxpayers continually bleed by them.

The list of environmental frauds is long and growing. Some subjects of costly fraud involve

- DDT
- Asbestos
- AIDS
- Endangered species
- Global warming
- Nuclear power

Fifty million victims of malaria, including forty million children, have died because of the DDT ban. That is twice the number of deaths initiated by Joseph Stalin against his own people. The Congress forced the corrupt EPA decision on the rest of the world with funding threats to UN agencies. South Africa has lifted its ban despite White House efforts to intervene (September 2008). Our government seeks to avoid yet another devastating foreign policy blowback.

Asbestosis and smoking go hand in hand. But asbestos took the blame. Asbestos must be removed from here and sequestered over there. It matters not where. It was a magnificent alibi for tearing down countless public buildings over a score of years and replacing them with landscaped campuses for the elite of society.

Up to a billion people were supposed to die of AIDS by the year 2000. A benign retrovirus (HIV) has been blamed. But AIDS remains confined to high risk groups that seek taxpayer paid medical care for their self inflicted syndrome. And just like surwage labor, they will seek out Democrats for a bailout.

On the left coast, the spotted owl decimated the timber industry. The endangered (not really) bird was a great alibi for tree huggers. Along the Olympic peninsula the forest service has been killing hatchery salmon. They are not wild. And in the Olympic interior the national park service seeks to kill mountain goats. They are not indigenous. Zealots prevail over common sense everywhere. And when their motives do not elicit the response they need they will invent new reasons for promoting their folly.

Global warming is potentially the greatest political con job and redistribution scheme in human history. Hitler would be impressed. So too would be his propaganda minister, Goebbels. The author must devote a page to this con.

Climate temperature fluctuations have correlated very well with fluctuations in solar activity over the last three hundred years that sunspot data has been recorded. No matter. Instead of attributing global warming to solar variation, the political left has faulted carbon dioxide emissions from burning fossil fuels.

The newly found Rosetta stone of global warmers, and Al Gore, is Antarctic ice core data (2005). This is wonderful data, but the political left misrepresents its meaning. The data correlates carbon dioxide levels with temperature levels over a 650 thousand year span. Ice core methane levels show the same correlation, but that elicits no intellectual response from the media dwarfs. Gore contends that carbon dioxide levels are a cause and that global warming is an effect.

But the resolution of the data does not reveal cause and effect. Temperature levels, carbon dioxide levels, and methane levels generally increase over long periods of time and then rather abruptly return to a baseline level. The correlation seems remarkable. Some natural process must periodically sweep carbon dioxide and methane from the Earth's atmosphere. Al Gore offers no explanation for their removal, but the author has one for you.

If variations in global temperatures cause carbon dioxide or other gases to escape from or return to some natural terrestrial reservoir, we have a cause and effect relation. But the cause over a time span of 650 thousand years is solar variability. It is not fossil fuel burning.

Climate fluctuations are readily attributable to changes in solar activity. And carbon dioxide increases are readily explained as an effect of global warming on sea temperature. The gas is extremely soluble in water. The concentration of carbon dioxide dissolved in sea water (2.2 percent) is nearly sixty times its 380 parts per million in the atmosphere.

The impurity that is the hardest to keep out of distilled water is carbon dioxide, which dissolves readily from the air.

Linus Pauling,

General Chemistry, Third edition
1970.

Carbon dioxide in huge amounts will diffuse out of sea water and reenter the atmosphere when the globe warms. So will methane. The grand correlation is natural and unremarkable (an inconvenient truth for Al Gore).

Recently (2008), pools of liquid carbon dioxide were reported sequestered in deep ocean trenches. It condenses under extreme sea pressure. We can assume that nature has been sequestering excess atmospheric carbon dioxide for epochs. The gas appears to shift between the troposphere and undersea reservoirs, driven by changes in global temperatures.

Global warming is merely another alibi employed by the barbarous left in their pursuit of wealth earned by others. Al Gore and his Kyoto Treaty would have Americans pay the third world for their gracious refusal to contribute to global warming (cap and trade). The third world shares the fruits of the industrial world through world trade but he ignores that. The treaty is a redistribution scheme of unsurpassed magnitude.

Wasn't it mentioned, somewhere, that the political left seeks to pull itself up by pulling others down?

The way the leftist media has sifted and selected the information that the public receives or is denied is both incriminating and illuminating.

Global warming or cooling is a natural phenomenon. It is not amenable to a political solution. But our energy shortage surely is. The cure is clean nuclear power. But Congressional collusion with environmentalists has demonized nuclear power and nuclear waste. The Congress painted itself into a corner with environmental lies. And now they must live the lie.

The production of nuclear energy and the recycling of nuclear waste have been proceeding for decades in France. There are no Chernobyl incidents to report and no multi billion dollar waste depositories hollowed out of the bowels of the Earth in France. In France the recycled waste is deposited in a single room under the floor of the La Hague plant in Normandy.

The monumental temple dug at Yucca Mountain in Nevada for the deposit of nuclear waste represents nothing but a monumental edifice to monumental political misfeasance, the political embrace of anti nuke hysteria.

One ten reactor Palo Verde (Arizona) power station would be the equivalent of twenty Hoover Dams in electrical power. Fifty power stations, at a capital cost of one trillion, could change the United States from an oil importer to an energy exporter.[39] Palo Verde was never completed. Environmentalists stopped construction at three reactors.

Organized labor, environmentalists, and unending lawsuits render energy independence impossible. Witness the economic destruction of the Washington Public Power Supply System (WPPSS) nuclear power project by organized labor circa 1973. In an unconscionable and totally despicable course of events, the unabated greed of labor unions and serial delays in construction by one strike after another bankrupted the consortium, destroyed retirement investments of the elderly, and ended the financing of nuclear power in America.

Private enterprise could readily finance the capital costs, but it wont, the political costs are insurmountable. This is your government at work!

Congressmen may ultimately spend trillions of dollars to bail out financial institutions it coerced into risky loans or bail out industries decimated by the organized labor they sired, but they will not embrace nuclear power or curb the greed of organized labor. They will fund windmills and other

---

[39] Cited from "Access to Energy," Vol 35, No 9, April 2008, Box 1250, Cave Junction, OR 97523.

losing alternatives to divert public attention from their prime role in creating energy shortages, wage gaps, and economic disaster.

Diversion of blame, hell yes! Resolution of the problems, hell no!

The electorate is initially exposed to political falsehoods in public schools. It can take years for the conditioned belief that politicians represent the people, to wash off. Politicians are career seekers. They enact legislation for zealots or opportunists who offer them campaign funds for their reelection. The evidence is overwhelming. We must examine the political indoctrination of public schools before we can ponder a way out of our crushing political environment.

Chapter 58

Political Indoctrination

Public education unions are second only to the legal monopoly in America in incumbent buying power. They are the largest labor monopoly surviving in America. The National Education Association (NEA) has 2.2 million members. The American Federation of Teachers (AFT) has 900,000.

The politicians and the education establishment have a great symbiosis. One can never spend too much tax money on schools. It's for the kids.

Yeah! Right!

AFT members in New York City are reported to work about four hours a day. You may note that if educators worked eight hours a day like the private sector, class sizes could immediately be cut in half.

A past president of the American Federation of Teachers answered a question about the welfare of kids by saying he will represent the kids when they start paying union dues.

In Illinois, an official of the Illinois Federation of Teachers admits that public pensions are creating anger in the private sector. He offers this solution.

Angry taxpayers should all join unions and negotiate better benefits for themselves.

Note the smooth but impossible solution offered for taxpayer resentment. Politicians will not negotiate with taxpayers. And taxpayers were not represented at the bargaining table.

Taxpayers must pay for public schools whether they educate or not, whether they have kids or not, whether their kids attend private schools or not, and whether the kids are illegal aliens or not.

Student Aptitude Tests have shown a long decline in student learning over decades.[40] The high school graduate today is just twelve years shy of the kind of education in history, math, science, and economics that he needs to discern the real political landscape encircling him.

Politicians abhor the thought of political and economic knowledge becoming public knowledge. That would reveal the great political lies that government engages in.

If the electorate had received a private education, it might recognize the tangled web of lies that politicians weave. It could learn of the economic destruction fathered by surwages. It could know the source of recessions and depression. It could know the enormous cost of public debt. It could know the political reason for inflation. It could know that minimum wage laws represent damage control and not altruism. It could know why crime has become an attractive alternative to actually earning a living. And the electorate might have avoided it.

If the electorate had received a private education, it could respect the profit motive. It could respect private property. It could admire entrepreneurs for their accomplishments and for the abundance they distribute to society. It could recognize corporations as wealth producers and not exploiters of labor. And it could know that abundant energy is the foundation of affluence.

If the electorate had received a private education, it could know that the natural economy will shift income taxes on people in economic demand to

---

[40] The tests were watered down (circa 2000) to convey an impression of improvement.

166

the consumer market in a free society. It could know that corporate taxes are passed to consumers. It could know that the only fair tax is a uniform retail sales tax. And it could know that all taxes are regressive and that taxation should be minimized.

If the electorate had been given a private education it could know that human progress and affluence are the products of free men engaging in free enterprise. It could know that government growth is destructive of progress and affluence.

Vouchers are not a solution. Organized labor in collusion with federal or state politicians will attach political strings to vouchers. They will demand that private schools hire union labor. The curriculum will be controlled.

The founders left education as an issue for the states or for the people. Public education was initiated by totalitarian states in Europe. Its alibi was to educate. Its purpose was to indoctrinate. It migrated west with Europeans.

The educational establishment denies students an understanding of the natural laws of economics and natural economic balance. The reader knows why.

The crimes at Columbine high school were committed by two young primitives who did not belong in school. They should have been released into the workforce at the age of puberty. Let them balance a longer career at lower income against a shorter career at higher income. But juvenile delinquents are incarcerated in public schools at the wish of organized labor.

Arrogance is taught as self esteem. Irresponsibility is taught as freedom. Lust among adolescents is tolerated and justified as natural. Nurseries are provided for unwed mothers. Our civil inheritance is downplayed or disparaged.

Global warming from fossil fuel use is an act to be deplored, oil companies are to be sued, endangered species (including cockroaches) are to be protected, and environmentalists are to be molded. In local news, Citizens for Environmental Education are denying that the schools are molding

167

environmental activists.[41] Do you recognize the threat, dear reader? There are no limits on government growth if government spending is not limited by Constitutional means.

Thomas Sowell, among others, has noted that many colleges and universities will graduate students with no courses required in English, economics, mathematics, or science. But courses are often required in the ideology of feminism, ethnicity, and gay pride.[42]

At this point the reader should be aghast at what politicians have done to the republic. The founders were men of honor. They risked their lives penning their names to the Declaration. They risked their lives to escape taxation without representation. Most politicians today are arrogant career seekers who will only risk the lives of others.

We must remove government from the educational landscape through a Constitutional amendment or an ignorant people will be enslaved to the state.

> **The Congress shall make no law favoring an establishment of education, or denying a freedom of curriculum.**

Will private cooperation arise to replace political coercion in the economic landscape? Will the children learn of individual rights? Will they learn of their political inheritance or will they lose it? Will an honest and civil society prevail or will the naked apes prevail? The jury is out.

---

[41] David Levesque, "Educators see red at charges of leaning green," cited in The Sun, 28 October 99.

[42] Thomas Sowell, "A college going soft for dollars," cited in The Sun, 03 July 99.

Part ix

Undoing the Political Damage

There is an old Libertarian saying. Politicians should be limited to two terms, one term in office and one term in jail. But term limits aren't going to happen. All the economic disasters of the twentieth century were initiated by Congressmen seeking political careers. They are not going to tolerate term limits. Their egregious efforts to remain incumbents at any cost to society must be redirected if taxpayers are to avoid a tyranny of poverty ruled by an elite class of wealthy predators.

Chapter 59

The Do Anything Congress

The Congress easily spends a trillion dollars (1000 billion) annually to ameliorate the damage created by earlier legislation. They cannot repeal a century of special interest legislation that is destroying our economic future. They can only throw good money after bad.

If our dysfunctional Congress was a dog, it would have been put out of its misery long ago.

No monarchy and its extended royal family could possibly cost as much as the United States Congress and its retinue of special interests.

The House of Bribes has failed to represent the taxpayer. James Madison would be appalled. In paper 54 of The Federalist, he wrote that the benefits and burdens (taxes) of government were to be bundled together by the method of apportionment of House seats. But liberal courts have wrongfully allowed the electorate to be separated into tax payers and tax beneficiaries.

The division in society is reflected by the two political parties in Congress. And the Congress is continuously engaged in deficit spending and in damage control. Let us briefly list what the do anything Congress has done.

- They have maximized tax seizure and minimized tax resistance by grossly invading personal privacy to determine an ability to pay.

- They have blocked with great lies and corrupt courts, attempts to place term limits on them.

- They have bashed the hopes and dreams of taxpayers by chaining them to huge interest payments on national debt in perpetuity.

- They collude with the feds to limit economic growth and bash the stock market.

- They collude with organized labor to move huge amounts of wealth from minimum paid labor to maximum paid labor.

- They appoint justices that infringe property rights for the purpose of increasing tax revenues.

- They have engaged in great lies about taxes.

- They have wrecked the gold standard and counterfeited paper notes in abundance creating perpetual inflation.

- They have given us the great depression, many recessions, and a certainty of economic disaster to come.

- They create monopolies while pretending to outlaw them.

- They curtail competition for campaign donations from the uncompetitive.

- They indoctrinate youth into political correctness by controlling public education.

- They curtail private education under the pretense of upholding freedom of religion.

- They curtail freedom of religion in public schools or buildings.

- They infringe our freedom of speech before an election.

- They seek to take from the taxpayer his right to bear arms.

- They engage in election rigging by gerrymandering congressional districts.

- They stack the courts to remove constitutional prohibitions on federal power.

And in an act of supreme arrogance,

- Private enterprise is blamed for federal destruction of the economy.

- The taxpayers are blamed for deficit spending and federal debt.

And the ways in which the Congress corrupts foreign policy and foments war has scarcely been explored. But the reader is protesting, get on with it!

The only way to curb the growth of destructive government is to handcuff growth with Constitutional limits on per annum spending.

If one cannot block the appetite, block the anus. A loss of appetite will follow.

When revenues from taxes, borrowing, outrageous fines and fees, confiscation, seizure, or business booms no longer determine the spending level, the politicians will trash the Byzantine revenue seeking structures they have erected, prioritize their spending, and abolish non productive programs. They will prosecute theft and encourage productivity just like the private sector.

Their appetite for revenue will be limited by restrictions on their ability to spend. And their appetite for buying power will cause them to quit inflating the money supply and cheapening the dollar. It could not get any better.

And of course the prohibition of unfunded mandates must be included in any constitutional constraint of federal spending or a miscreant Congress will mandate the states to fund their treachery.

Once the surwages and entitlements of favored interests are removed from the federal landscape, state landscapes should improve as well. Once political impediments are removed, a free people will initiate improvement.

> **I hold it, that a little rebellion, now and then, is a good thing, and as necessary in the political world as storms in the physical.**
>
> --Thomas Jefferson--

Chapter 60

The Electorate

"We have met the enemy and he is us," exclaimed Pogo the cartoon possum in the popular comic strip of the same name.

Society is a mix of predators and prey. That is the reality. The only way to form a prosperous and civil society under such conditions is to constrain the predators. Normally a threat of retribution from a populace exercising their right to bear arms, will keep predators at bay. Unfortunately, many predators today use the power of government to facilitate their aggression and taxpayers or consumers are their prey. And they want their prey disarmed.

The founders had opposite intentions. The government was to represent tax payers. Their intentions are obvious from the way in which the Constitution apportions seats in the House of Representatives. Those not taxed are not to be counted in the apportionment of house seats to the states within the union.

What part of <u>not taxed</u> and <u>not counted</u> does the Supreme Court not understand?

In the beginning, members of the Senate were appointed by their state legislatures. Senate careers did not depend on campaign finance. The influence of special interests, beyond that of state interests, was negligible. In 1913 the seventeenth amendment exposed the Senate to the need for campaign funds and the greed of organized labor. Big mistake! In 1914 Congress ceded their independence to big labor in return for a political career.[43]

In the beginning the members of the House of Representatives limited themselves to two terms (four years) of office. But in the depression era, the political left in the House initiated the pursuit of Congressional careers. Today damn few will limit their terms.

---

[43] Clayton Act

And when the people of several states tried to resurrect term limits on their Representatives in the nineties, the Supreme Court blocked their attempt.

The Congress has divided the people into tax payers and tax beneficiaries by pursuing political careers. Dividing the people, irregardless of intent, is a fatal step for a political union and the founders would have known better.

But dividing the people elicits campaign donations. The electorate is being asked to make decisions beyond their knowledge and competence. The electorate has no aggregate knowledge that would qualify a majority to make intelligent choices in many matters placed before it. How could it where only the few possess the requisite experience or expertise and the many are brainwashed by government education. But dragging the electorate into the question raises passion and campaign funds and the Congress can blame the electorate for all problems.

An electorate can only make aggregate decisions. And it does that superbly by its participation as buyers and sellers (demand and supply) in a free economy. But aggregate knowledge is diffuse. It cannot be focused into expertise.

Greed prevails over need when armed by law. This is the quintessential problem with government. It is imperative that all voters in a republic be taxpayers and that only taxpayers vote. It is also imperative that taxes are limited by a Constitutional limit on total spending because government never earns its income by pleasing customers. Government seizes income at its pleasure.

A few dozen seats out of four hundred thirty five in the House of Representatives may be competitive in an election. The rest are owned by one of two political parties. And the losers gain political appointments. Political careers are more or less permanent. But their costs are appalling. The Congress has been the source of unconscionable economic destruction for a century. Can they admit to misfeasance and bribery, banish the conflicts they have nurtured, and rescind corrupt legislation?

They cannot! The Congress in the aggregate knows nothing. And as individuals they can admit to nothing. Their careers have top priority. They can only fail to do what duty requires (nonfeasance). But before the Congress drags America down into the third world, maybe the taxpayers could initiate a sea change in the way the Congress operates by offering a humongous bribe of their own.

Chapter 61

Restoring the Republic

The Preamble to the Constitution enumerates several reasons for ordaining and establishing the Constitution. To 'promote the general welfare' was one those reasons. The preamble was written before the tenth amendment which clearly forbids an expansive interpretation of federal power. Therefore the preamble is not a grant of power; it merely expresses the intent of 'We the People'.

'General welfare' appears in the body of the Constitution in Article I. Section 8, where the enumerated powers granted to the Congress appear. If promoting the general welfare was an unbound grant of power instead of a limitation, why bother with a list of enumerated powers? Why insert the tenth amendment?

Nevertheless, by 1937 the Congress had assumed unlimited powers to ameliorate the economic depression that their corrupt legislation had brought upon the American people. Liberal justices have further divided the people by allowing government to favor tax beneficiaries with benefits while it excludes tax payers from them. They have divided the people and threatened American unity. And it is all justified by a corruption of two words, general welfare.

Since government beneficiaries and tax payers are no longer the same entities as the founders intended, taxes are out of control.

The total amount of money the government is authorized to spend per annum must be fixed in Constitutional Law. That will stop government from rendering the dollar worthless on the world market as happened to Russia and the ruble.

A century of cheapening the value of the dollar will end when a per annum spending limit goes into effect. Surwages, unearned entitlements, damage control in perpetuity, bailouts in perpetuity, and debt payments in perpetuity will not be tolerated when federal politicians feel the same constraints that taxpayers struggle with daily.

But how can taxpayers get a constitutional limit on per annum spending? The problem is systemic. Congressional careers depend on the feed and care of tax beneficiaries.

There may be a way. One chamber of the Congress could be severed from their ties to election campaign donors. They could be given an indefinite political career upon winning their election to office.

Once elected, they could be free of special interest influence or threat. Once elected, they could be immune to bribery. Once elected, they could answer only to the Constitution they swear to uphold. Careers will sever them from their continuous need for bribes. This is a political imperative. It must be done.

The Constitution reads,

> **The President, Vice President, and all civil Officers of the United States, shall be removed from Office on Impeachment for, and Conviction of, Treason, Bribery, or other high Crimes and Misdemeanors.**

The founders considered bribery a crime on the level of treason. They could not have foreseen the legalization of influence money by campaign reform laws in the twentieth century.

Congressmen will do anything for a career. So why not offer them the ultimate bribe. The electorate could offer them a <u>legitimate</u> career.

Once elected, the members of a career chamber must avoid the appearance of bribery. Once seated, the acceptance of gratuities from lobbyists must be treated by the justice department as a potential bribe. It could not be campaign funding.

A legitimate career can cut the strings between campaign donors and their Congressional puppets. But to keep the electorate in control of their Congress after the strings are cut, the electorate must possess a trump card.

The electorate must be given Constitutional authority to remove the entire membership of the House from political careers for life for nonfeasance in office. A vote on the question might be held every two years. A majority of Congressional districts (218 or more) could oust the entire House in a truly bipartisan manner. Congressional elections could then seat 435 new faces. This political career ending threat could force all members to represent society as a whole instead of engaging in continuous class warfare and damage control.

It is important that politicians once removed from the House be removed from political careers for life. Otherwise they will simply seek reelection or political appointment (as they do today) and continue their nonfeasance in office. The House of Bribes must be taken from the criminals and returned to the people.

A legitimate political career cannot be a greater threat than the illegitimate political careers of today. The Congressional puppets must be freed from their life support systems and the electorate as a whole made their true and lasting concern. Fortunately the Roosevelt experience induced Americans to put term limits on the presidency.

While an ignorant electorate may never agree on cause and effect, they may nevertheless be able to force a sea change upon the Congress in the manner in which representatives pursue political careers. The class warfare will end when a majority of the Congress can no longer remain in office <u>by dividing the people.</u>

Limits on election contributions will not be needed when campaign contributors are promoting the public good instead of investing in political larceny. Career members of a chamber could rise above the influence of bribes. When one chamber is immunized, it can move the other in a positive direction.

A bribe taking Congress cannot make the initial step. But a career House may move the country away from the economic abyss that career seeking has created.

A constitutional freeze on per annum spending is the <u>initial</u> step to halting the developing economic disaster. That could immediately appreciate the dollar and reduce the sting of a default of the national debt. The bashing of the economy could cease. Velocity could rise to its natural limit at full employment. And when the seizure of income under color of law ceases, minimum wages will soar, wage gaps will narrow to an optimum spread, and charity can replace the insatiable appetite of public welfare.

The question remains. Was Thomas Jefferson right? Are rebellions now and then a necessary and good thing?

Major economic disasters have been precipitated by the political pursuit of careers in the Congress. Greater economic disasters are in the government pipeline. They will flower in the new millennium, if their roots in special interest fertilizer are not cut and cut soon.

A democracy must be constrained from looting the wealth of their fellow men. An electorate that <u>earns</u> its wealth in private enterprise would respect the labor of others. And a Congress free of biennial threats may resume its Constitutional duty of representing the taxpayer and enforcing human rights.

The looting of their fellow men is exactly what the pushers of a graduated income tax attempt to do. Private enterprise evaded the attempt. But it was naturally evaded by a reduction in the number of professionals in the landscape and by a rising of the costs for their services. A civil society would not have tolerated the attempt or suffered the unintended economic consequences.

Actually, the American people did not approve the income tax. Many of the states had attached conditions to be met before they would accept such an amendment. The Taft administration ignored their conditional approval, <u>counted them all as yeas</u>, and his Secretary of State arbitrarily ruled the amendment ratified.

Taft was later appointed Chief Justice of the Supreme Court. How convenient! He was put in a position to block any legal challenge to the corrupt ratification process he presided over while in the White House.

A civil society recognizes a difference between charity and thievery. In charity, the donor determines the amount given. In theft, the recipient determines the amount taken. Charity is the hallmark of a free people residing in an affluent and civil society. The political left is far from fairness or charity. Do not confuse their alibis with altruism. Their primal instinct is to pull themselves up by pulling others down.

Epilogue

Did Marx know that in extolling the redistribution of wealth he was promoting theft? I have given Marx the benefit of the doubt by calling him a moron instead of a thief. But among predators, greed is a much stronger instinct than is an unselfish concern for the welfare of others.

Labor unions engage in coercion. Strikers behave in a belligerent and malicious manner on a picket line. They are there to intimidate competitive labor (no altruism found here). They employ vicious and intimidating language at the bargaining table. They are there only to make demands and threaten employers with huge economic losses in a strike (no altruism found here either).

But entrepreneurs, doctors, scientists, and others, compete as individuals earning a better living on their own. They are not collectivized. They are not malicious. They are not demanding. They are simply in demand. It is consumer demand that raises their income instead of threats.

In a free society people are free to pursue a better wage through education and training. That is what should be done. Seizing surwages from an employer by the employee cannot be made right by organizing into a collective. It is only made legal in the predator society.

There is a difference between wages and profit. Supply and demand will determine the market value of labor. The entrepreneur must pay it. If the laborer wants to share an entrepreneurial profit, he must stop earning wages and start paying them. Entrepreneurs are not hogging the wealth. They are producing it.

From each in accordance with his ability, to each in accordance with his need, sing the socialist thieves. One must rise by pulling another down.

But the socialist is wrong. Wealth is not the product of labor. Wealth is the product of entrepreneurs who provide the means and orchestrate the fusion of labor, technology, material, and energy. Without the orchestration, there is no wealth. There is merely labor. There is only the hunter and the gatherer.

There is but an empty landscape inhabited by primitives.

Inverse Algebraic Relations

An inverse relation between two dependent variables means that when one of the variables increases in value, the other must decrease in value. The value of one variable is tied inversely to the other. The relationship may be expressed algebraically as the product of two variables.

$$x \, y = n$$

The equation reads that the value of **x** times the value of **y** equals the value of **n**.

The variables that are inversely dependent are x and y. The product of the variables is n. The value of n is normally a constant. That is it is a fixed quantity.

If the value of x were to increase then the value of y must decrease to maintain the same product. If the value of x were quartered then the value of y must quadruple. The variables may assume different sets of values, but their product must remain the same if they are inversely dependent.

If one were to plot on a graph all sets of x and y (numbers which multiplied together give the same product n), all sets would lie on a curve with an appearance as shown. This portion of the algebraic function is the graphical signature of a true inverse relationship.

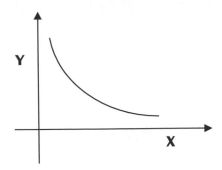

The shape of the curve shown is that of a rectangular hyperbola. Note that as one follows the curve down and to the right the value of x at any point increases and the corresponding value of y decreases.

An economic demand curve shows an inverse relation between the cost of an object and the numbers sold. Most economic texts show demand curves as straight lines trending downward to the right. It is important to appreciate the difference.

A demand curve can display the price of widgets on the vertical scale vice the number of sales at each price on the horizontal scale. As prices fall the quantity sold at each price will rise. This is a well known inverse relation. But it is not the one we seek.

A straight line may be a reasonable approximation for an inverse relation on a widget scale. But a straight line requires the product of price times quantity sold to rise substantially in mid range. Thus the money supply is quite elastic.

A hyperbola, in contrast, requires that the amount of money paid (n) does not appreciably change within the range of the variables x and y. And we must hold the product n constant because we are going to make n represent the national money supply about which the variables are related. And the national money supply is quite inelastic in comparison. It is subject only to federal diddling.

If we divide both sides of our equation by **x** we maintain the inverse relation but separate the dependent variables. The equation reads that the value of **y** equals the value of n divided by the value of **x**.

$$y = n\,/\,x$$

The separation of variables expresses the inverse relationship in the form of the Equation of Inflation and in the form of the Equation of Employment that the author introduced earlier in the book. Prices and aggregate production are inversely related by an inelastic money supply. Wage rates and employment are inversely related for the same reason. And the numerator (**n**) in each inverse relation represents the money supply.

One must note that x and y in our equation remain inversely related even if the money supply inflates. The vertical scale (wages or prices) will inflate with the money supply. But its inverse relation with the horizontal scale (employment or production) remains for any value of n.

Think of the relationship between x and y as that of two children on opposite ends of a seesaw. When one rises the other must fall.

Think of inflation as raising the center of the seesaw in elevation. Irregardless of the change in elevation, the children remain in an inverse relationship with each other. One must rise if the other falls.

Average prices remain inversely proportional to aggregate production (all products are sold) and average wages remain inversely proportional to man hours of employment, irregardless of political interference with the nation's money supply (the value of n). This economic truism is reflected in the first two laws of Economics in a Nutshell.

The evidence of political interference with the inverse laws of economics is inflation (increasing the money supply), stagflation (increasing the money supply and the surwages of labor), widening wage gaps (increasing surwages or progressive taxes), recessions (decreasing the money supply or increasing surwages or taxes), and depression (collapse of the money supply and the hogging of surwages by those remaining employed).

It is the inverse relationship that is of paramount importance to understanding the economics of inflation, stagflation, wage gaps, recession, and depression. They arise out of futile Congressional efforts to override two naturally occurring inverse economic relationships and with Federal Reserve efforts to counter the unintended consequences by diddling with the money supply.

The Composition of Dissolved Air in Water

Atmospheric gases dissolve in liquids in proportion to their partial pressure in air and in accordance with their solubility in the liquid. The solubility of nitrogen in water at zero degrees Centigrade is 23.54 ml/l. That of oxygen is 48.89 ml/l. That of carbon dioxide is a remarkable 1713 ml/l.

If air consists of about 21 percent oxygen, 79 percent nitrogen, and 380 parts per million of carbon dioxide, the volume of the dissolved gases in water at one atmosphere and zero degrees Centigrade is,

Nitrogen   (23.54 ml/l) (0.79) = 18.60 ml/l.
Oxygen   (48.89 ml/l) (0.21) = 10.27 ml/l.
Carbon dioxide   (1713 ml/l) (0.000380) = 0.651 ml/l.

The volume of dissolved air in water is then 18.60+10.27+0.651 or 29.52 ml per liter.

The percent of nitrogen is 100 times the ratio (18.60) / (29.52) or 63%.
That of oxygen is 100 times the ratio (10.27) / (29.52) or 34.8%.
That of carbon dioxide is 100 times the ratio (0.651) / (29.52) or 2.2%.

The ratio of carbon dioxide in dissolved air to that in atmospheric air is nearly sixty to one.

$$CO2 / CO2 = (0.022) / (0.000380) = 57.89$$

Real air has water vapor and many other ingredients at minute partial pressures. Their minute presence will not appreciably affect the ratio derived for CO2. The ratio illuminates the capacity of global seas to swallow up or release atmospheric carbon dioxide under the influence of solar cooling or warming. This immediate effect occurs at the air/sea interface.

And at abyssal depths sea pressure rains excess CO2 into pools for epochal storage. The mere presence of liquid carbon dioxide sequestered at deep ocean depths suggests that our global ocean is primarily responsible for removing and limiting the atmospheric abundance of carbon dioxide.